CHRIS SPICER

The Reel Story

TEN MOVIES THAT SUM UP MY LIFE

malcolm down

PUBLISHING

CONTENTS

CONTENTS

RECOMMENDATIONS

"In a culture where 'stories' have become the primary means of communicating information, heritage and truth, Chris Spicer has chosen the perfect way to let us 'see behind the scenes' of his life! In *The Reel Story*, his love for movies come alive as he takes us on an exploration of 10 classic movies where we discover the timeless and profound wisdom hidden within the screenwork of skilled actors and writers. What a brilliant way to let us see ourselves! Most of our media is a reflection of our realities, both good and bad. That's why I'd suggest we all can 'look and learn' from Chris in this wonderful life story! Enjoy the journey!"

Bishop Tony Miller – Senior Pastor, The Gate Church, Oklahoma, USA

"In *The Reel Story*, Chris Spicer tells the story of his life through the lens of ten movies that have moved and shaped him and his family. These ten films act as windows onto experiences as wide-ranging as spiritual abuse (a very hot topic right now) and approval addiction, both of which the author has confronted in his life. As a movie lover myself, I cannot recommend this book more highly. Chris's insight into films, as well as his honesty about his own past, has created a compelling, celluloid memoir that doesn't try to hide the cellulite."

Mark Stibbe – Film critic and author of *A Passion for the Movies*

"Since the first frame of film went through a camera more than 100 years ago, movies have challenged, angered, motivated and inspired millions of people. In *The Reel Story*, Chris Spicer has found ten of those movies and explored how they impacted his life, and how they can change ours. If you love great stories, you'll love this book. It's a powerful reminder that film has the remarkable ability to be a mirror that changes our perspective on everything."

Phil Cooke PhD – Filmmaker, media consultant and author of *Unique: Telling Your Story in the Age of Brands and Social Media*

"I have often said, watch *Dead Poets Society*, *Good Will Hunting* and *Mr. Holland's Opus* and you will meet my eldest son. If the list of movies in Chris's content was DNA, I'd almost think we are related. My son is also an opera buff! If Chris ever writes an operatic version, I really will get nervous. To make matters worse, he includes *Shawshank Redemption* and I'm a retired prison governor. So, congratulations on the book, my long-lost relative!"

Paul Manwaring – Senior Leadership team at Bethel Church, Redding, California, USA

"Irene and I share Chris and Tina's passion for films. As we have gotten older, we seldom have a cinema night out without tears or laughter. We have found these responses to be therapeutic and healing due to our own joys and sorrows of life. Thank you for this transparent and honest invitation to read and feel your story."

Stuart Bell – Senior Pastor of Alive Church, Lincoln, and Leader of Ground Level Network

"This book is profound, prophetic, poignant and greatly needed, not to say challenging. It holds up a mirror to the human condition and the contemporary church and when I looked into that mirror, I invariably saw myself. Scary! Honest and non-judgemental, *The Reel Story* has laugh out loud moments and is so easy to relate to."

Amanda Kay – Copsewood Editorial Services Ltd

"Chris brilliantly weaves in life experiences and lessons he has learnt, both naturally and spiritually, intertwined with the plots and characters of a variety of movies. It's a 'one of a kind' book that will hold the reader's interest and give much food for thought. Well done!"

Roxy Iverson – Ministers Fellowship International, Portland, Oregon

"*The Reel Story* will make you laugh, cry and most of all think! Chris's novel approach to revealing his life's journey through ten great films, offers an amazing insight into the life he has lived and the lessons learnt along the way – so make yourself comfortable, grab yourself some popcorn and settle down with great book!"

Adrian Hurst – Senior Minister, Oasis Church, Birmingham

"Chris Spicer gives his autobiography a unique spin, weaving it around his favourite movies. But what makes this book really special is there aren't many people who spend half a century in ministry – and even less with the honesty to then share both their victories and their mess ups (lessons learnt) so that others can learn. He really does Keep It Reel."

Roger Blackmore – Lead Pastor, Genesis Church, New York

"From the title to the creative layout, this book grabs your attention. Difficult to put down, the more you read, the more you to want to read. Using an eclectic mix of movies, the author draws you into his life. With its fascinating storyline, this book connects both writer and reader alike in a journey of discovery. *The Reel Story* is an honest, vulnerable, unique and healing book."

John King – Founding Pastor of Riverside Community Church, Peoria, IL, USA

"*The Reel Story* is a beautiful and deeply personal expression of the learning that God has imparted to Chris in his years as a father, husband and church leader. The use of film narratives to cleverly weave together lessons learned make the book an absorbing and easy read. I was profoundly moved by the powerful and honest moments of weakness and failure, as well as challenged by consistent call to follow Christ and be the person I was made to be. A thoroughly enjoyable and worthwhile read."

Tim Cross – Senior Pastor, River Church, London

"Whether people of one faith, all faiths or no faith at all, we all use a code to govern the way we live life. Chris Spicer has been able to find a resonance in these amazing movies to the Christian life he has led, which makes this book both poignant and important. Everyone is looking for purpose and hope. It should be no surprise that these core messages of the Christian faith can be found alive and well in places that look nothing like a church!"

Andrew Edmiston – Managing Director, I.M. Group Ltd, UK

"This book is written in a unique and engaging style that helps the reader travel through Chris's favourite films revealing the insights of Chris and his family's journey over the past years . . . lessons learnt through decisions and deceptions open each of us to a life journey where the wonders and pitfalls of ministry can lead both to blessing and pain! Each chapter leads us into another cave of discovery revealing a life truth which ultimately leads to hope . . . a must read for anyone who dares to win."

Gary Spicer – Senior Pastor, Mosaic Church, Coventry, UK

ACKNOWLEDGEMENTS

I am sincerely grateful to Mark Stibbe and the good folks at BookLab (www.thebooklab.co.uk) for editing *The Reel Story*. Without their work, this publication would probably never have seen the light of day. A big thank you to Malcolm Down and his team who believed enough in *The Reel Story* to take it through the publishing process. Thanks also to Taffy Davies for his excellent illustrations that appear throughout this book. Without his artistic skills, neither this book nor www.coffeechats.org would have the creative 'draw' they have. Thanks also to my daughter Hannah for the book cover design. Finally, I would like to add my heartfelt thanks to my wife Tina. Without her love, patience and constant companionship over the last fifty years of trailblazing and pioneering adventure, this story would not have been possible.

DEDICATION
To my rock-star grandchildren

INTRODUCTION

Leaving Nothing Unsaid

Could a visit to the cinema be literally what the doctor ordered? The idea that films can offer us a healthy dose of the feel-good-factor is perhaps more credible than you might think. When Dr Norman Cousins was diagnosed with a degenerative disease, he took the decision to check out of the hospital and into a hotel across the street. Along with high levels of Vitamin C, he prescribed for himself a continuous drip-feed of comedy films. Although his ailment was no laughing matter, he later said that ten minutes of laughter would give him two hours of pain-free sleep.[1] His story suggests that *reel* therapy might be real after all.

Some movies have more than just entertainment value. They have the capacity to restore your soul. You can be having a horrible day, a stressful time in your life, but a visit to the cinema can improve your mental and emotional health. Releasing happy hormones, it is particularly comic movies that can improve your state of mind and make you feel better about yourself, and those around you too.

Not that my family ever needed convincing of this; the fact that my wife and I have produced a family of film buffs probably tells you a lot about our parenting style. Even today, when bringing an end to a heated marital discussion, my wife Tina will simply say, along with the correct hand gestures, "You can do this with me, or you can do it without me."[2]

---

1. Blog by Sebastian Gendry, "Norman Cousins Anatomy of an Illness", www.laughteronlineuniversity.com.
2. Based on a saying from the 2010 movie, *Knight and Day*, starring Tom Cruise and Cameron Diaz.

Watching films made raising four children with a twelve-year age difference far easier than it might have been otherwise. As our kids grew up, our common love of all things cinematic began to morph into a unique form of movie-orientated language. Much to the bewilderment of visitors, we could conduct whole conversations using nothing more than key phrases from the world of cinema and screen. This blockbuster banter would be somewhat disconcerting for first-time guests.

When it came to a family film night, everyone had his or her personal preference.

While the girls might insist on another viewing of *Pride and Prejudice* (2005), *While You Were Sleeping* (1995) or *Sleepless in Seattle* (1993), the boys would argue for a rerun of the *Star Wars Trilogy* or the latest Bond film. "Anything but another chick flick," they would say. In scenes akin to *Gunfight at the O.K. Corral* (1957), everyone would face their opponent down with his or her choice. All this for a quiet evening spent in with the family.

When it came to a family member's rite of passage into the Spicer tribe, the initiation ceremony would undoubtedly include at least one viewing of Tina's all-time favourite film, *What About Bob?* (1991) More about that later!

I'm sure you get the point: we are a family of movie lovers and film buffs. That's why I've chosen to tell the story of my life using ten movies that have made a big impact on me and my family. That isn't as easy as it sounds when there are so many timeless classics, so many films that have added not just fun but also meaning to my life.

If you could choose ten movies to showcase your life and send a message to future generations, what would they be? Perhaps, like me, you would provide an eclectic mix of favourite films. *The Reel Story* is my collection of film-based, autobiographical stories. I really hope you enjoy them.

Each of the ten films in the ten chapters that follow outlines the *lessons learnt* and *mistakes made* from a lifetime in business, social enterprise, education and various branches of Christianity. Each movie illustrates timeless truths I want to pass onto future generations. More than a rerun of golden oldies, this is a contemporary way of narrating about those people, objects and events that have either *mugged* me or *ministered* to me in a journey lasting what in biblical terms is "three score years and ten".[3] From middle England to Midwest America, from an English seaport to the coastline of Portland, Oregon, from British social housing to Brazilian shanty towns, *The Reel Story* provides some of the highlights of the adventure of my life.

While some of you may know me as a father or grandfather, others will know me as a work colleague, businessman, church leader, educator, author or public speaker. Few of you will know the real person behind the persona.

So, before the main feature begins, let me give you a trailer composed of a few, key background facts about my life. Born in 1946, I am the second son of Thomas Rudolf and Winifred May Spicer, two loving parents who brought me up in the city of Coventry after World War Two.

While my parents showed me love, my community taught me life.

Family and friends would tell me stories about scary nights when women and children huddled in a dank metal air raid

---

3. Psalm 90:10, KJV.

shelter half-submerged in the back garden, while the nightly patrols, performed by men unable to do active service, watched out for incendiary bombs falling on neighbours' properties. Neighbours recalled the willingness of people to share what meagre food rations they had, and the readiness of others to offer a listening ear and a shoulder to soak the tears. Those five years of war created a village-like mentality in the suburbs of the bombed city of my birth.

Mine was a community in which policing was not a problem. When adolescents got out of hand, the 'village elders' took care of it. Family friends became surrogate aunts and uncles whom you ignored at your peril. Unlocked doors were the norm, public telephones a necessity and neighbourhood communication a chat over the garden fence. Common sense was common and adult authority unquestioned.

As an aside here, I can't help thinking that the contemporary Church might learn a lot from this part of my story. Instead of having religious gatherings in alien buildings and environments, perhaps what's needed is a return to an understanding of Christianity as people doing life together, helping each other in practical ways, supporting each other through the storms of life, watching out for one another in the war between light and darkness. This would provide a welcome and much needed antidote to the pandemic of social loneliness in our world and create a sense of belonging in the presence of the Father who "sets the lonely in families".[4] Just a thought!

Anyway, back to my story. Far from being perfect, my parents tried their best to avoid the same mistakes their parents had made. But like every subsequent generation, in their pursuit of parental excellence, they managed to create their own catalogue of errors.

---

4. Psalm 68:6.

Thomas Spicer, or Tom to his friends, was a man of few words. A practical fixer of problems, his carpentry skills were much in demand. Tom would often rob himself of potential profit in pursuit of his business motto: *Your satisfaction is my advertisement.* The pleasure of a job well done was my father's objective. Besides the pursuit of perfection and a great work ethic, my father gave me a love of fishing, drawing, carpentry and anything automobile related. A gentle giant who preferred to leave the talking and disciplining to his wife, Dad led the way in showing me the importance of the phrase, "If a job is worth doing, it's worth doing well."

Winifred, or Winnie as she was known, was a loving mother who ensured her children had a great upbringing. Although not a matriarch, Mum was clearly the power behind the throne. While Dad did the manual labour, Mum managed the home and, when needed, administered the discipline. Whether a smack at home or the slipper at school, corporal punishment was an integral part of my childhood education. It became a normal and acceptable part of the *seat* of learning for me. And before the liberals go off on one, no it did not create any lasting emotional damage. The discipline I received was proportionate to the wrong I had done. And although neither of my parents was perfect, I can categorically say that I am what I am by the grace of God and the gift of two loving parents.

Living on the edge of a local mining community in the automobile capital of the Western world, cars, coal and chapel life were an integral part of my childhood.

Men returning from war came to our community with both mining expertise and, equally important, a desire for chapel life. What began as a small 'Cottage Meeting' soon outgrew the small end-terrace house and was forced to relocate to a prefabricated tin hut. Although the building owed more to army surplus than architectural splendour, this was where I was introduced to church life and the Christian faith. The hard, wooden benches, feeble lighting, poor heating and basic toilet amenities had little to attract members of the public, but the spiritual fervour and warm welcome was enough to draw a crowd. We may have lacked the sandstone exterior, stained glass windows and impressive spire of St Thomas C. of E. Church, but the Keresley Heath Mission Hall created a great sense of belonging. And once inside, when the distraught tones of an old pump organ were sounded, the congregation needed little encouragement to worship. It was here that I soon discovered that the benches made a perfect drawing surface for up-and-coming artists. While my parents listened to the dulcet tones of the Reverend George Waring as he preached, others of us practised our artistic skills.

A soft-spoken Welsh orator, George Waring was a kind-hearted man who loved to serve people. A short, silvery haired man, George found time to lead a growing congregation while having a full-time job in the mines. He was clearly a man who heard from God. When he passed, we all mourned. Three days before his untimely death, this much-loved minister requested that my brother and I visit him. Confined to his bed through some mining-related illness, he had already spoken to our mother in vague terms about a dream that included my brother and me. He had asked to see us as soon as possible. "What was the Pastor's dream? Was it like those that the biblical Joseph had, in which he saw his older brothers bowing down before him?" Whatever it was, we will never know. Just hours before our proposed visit, the Reverend George Waring passed peacefully from this life to the next.

Maybe this traumatic loss is what lies behind my deep desire expressed in the phrase, 'Leaving Nothing Unsaid'. Maybe that's why I'm so keen to tell my story. But a word of warning here: our life stories aren't the same as the stories told in films. Although we might prefer our story to have a classic beginning and a fairy tale ending, the truth is, our beginnings can be messy, our endings can be imperfect. More than that, our stories don't fall neatly into one simple category. Life is a mixture of comedy, fantasy, romance, tragedy, and so on. While some might prefer to edit their past, massage their present and fantasise about their future, an honest person would admit that their story is full of lessons learnt and mistakes made. That is why I am not going to photoshop the ugly parts of my life or glamorise the mundane bits either. Even though I shall be referring to films, *The Reel Story* is an opportunity to tell my story in a non-idealised way, to pass on the lessons learnt from failure as well as success while studying at the university of life.

Whether our existence is a legacy to be remembered, or a liability from which to recover, each of us forms part of a chapter in the autobiography of other people.

The mere mention of our names will create a mixture of memories in the memoirs of those who took the time to journey with us. *The Reel Story* is my story of those people, objects and events that have influenced my life. I have written it to inspire the next generation to run faster and go further than my generation ever thought possible, and to offer a word of warning about those distractions, detours and diversions that can bring ruin to the unsuspecting traveller.

As in the biblical story of the Good Samaritan, I have been *mugged* by some and *marginalised* by others during my spiritual journey. But rather than react negatively, which is my natural tendency, I want to try to be positive and celebrate those who have *ministered* to me. Some are listed in the end credits of this publication; they are the true champions of my story.

So, then, find yourself a comfy seat and enjoy the movies I've selected, ten films that form the backdrop for the adventure of a lifetime.

CHAPTER

TRAILER

Dead Poets Society (1989) tells the story of a teacher in a boys' boarding school. Played by Robin Williams, John Keating comes to teach English at a conservative and elitist school, the fictional Welton Academy. It is 1959 and Keating has set his sights on inspiring his pupils through his love of poetry and his highly unorthodox but extremely effective teaching methods. Himself a Welton alumnus, Keating tells his young acolytes to make their lives extraordinary. Discovering that Keating was a member of the Dead Poets Society when he was at the school, one of the pupil's decides to resurrect the club. All this attracts the attention and wrath of the strict headteacher, Gale Nolan, who, in the end, fires Keating, but not before Keating's students have hailed him as "O Captain! My Captain!" In this chapter, we look at the importance of teachers in our lives. While all teachers are *instructors*, very few are *investors*. Keating exemplifies the *investor* type. He is the kind of teacher who brings the shy guy – played in the movie by Ethan Hawke – out of their shells. He is a lasting embodiment of 'The Keating Effect'.

THE KEATING EFFECT

Dead Poets Society

There were six words that always seemed to summarise my end-of-year report: "Works hard but could try harder." They capture my whole educational experience. Yet these were my formative years, the opening chapter of a life featuring some extraordinary teachers who saw potential in me that others didn't. These teachers fell into one of two categories, hard-line *instructors* or heartfelt *investors*. The former filled your mind with information; the latter transformed your life through inspiration.

While the instructors were cold and calculated, the investors were warm and affirming.

With their high educational demands and expectations, instructors would make withdrawals from your bank of self-belief and leave you feeling emotionally bankrupt. Investors, on the other hand, deposited a level of self-confidence that left you feeling richer. Handing out facts and figures at an alarming rate, my instructors hoped I would remember enough of the right information to achieve good grades. To the instructor, success was a grade to achieve, rather than a life to develop. Investors somehow managed to lift me up from where I was and pointed me to a higher level, which they believed I could attain. Brokers in self-belief, these men and women enabled me to see beyond the horizon of my perceived limitations. They walked alongside me, travelling with me to the land of possibility.

Although the number of investors was few, I echo the words of the Apostle Paul when he stated, "I am what I am [by] the grace of God."[5] I would reverently add, I am what I am by the grace of God and because of the goodness of those who believed in me enough to invest time, energy and resources in my educational development. While some teachers leave a legacy to enjoy, others leave a liability to unlearn. True investors are noted as much for their positive attitude as they are for their personal aptitude.

The American author and leadership guru John Maxwell would often begin a class on 'Attitudes' by asking his listeners to name four of the greatest influencers in their life. He would then ask them to choose one of the following three words that best characterises their choice.

Appearance, their dress code or physical appearance.

Aptitude, their knowledge, skills or abilities.

Attitude, their positive angle of approach to life.

On every occasion, the highest score always went to those influencers known for their *attitude,* their positive angle of approach to people, objects and events.

Perhaps, this is the reason I love teacher/student movies like *Goodbye Mr. Chips* (1939/1969); *Dead Poets Society* (1989); *Mr. Holland's Opus* (1995); *Pay it Forward* (2000); *Finding Forrester* (2000) and *Freedom Writers* (2007). All of these are arguably *good* movies. But greatness belongs to the two movies that bookend *The Reel Story.* These are *Dead Poets Society* and *Mr. Holland's Opus.* Although one of the most overly used one-liners of the late 1980s and early 1990s, the phrase 'carpe diem'

---

5. 1 Corinthians 15:10, ESV.

spoke of making the most of time, something that as adolescents or young adults we often ignore. 'Carpe diem' taught us that the brevity of life is something we should never underestimate. Following my mother's premature death, I found a similar sentiment scribbled in her Bible. Next to the New Testament verse that reads, "For what is life? It is even a vapour, that appeareth for a little time, and then vanisheth away",[6] Winifred May Spicer had written just two words: "*Little time.*" These proved to be prophetic; at the age of 57, Mum suffered a heart attack and died. Time is a precious commodity we ignore at our peril. If Mr. Keating's lesson in the lobby of Welton School tells us anything, it is to live every day as if it were our last.

Change Agents

What makes a great movie? Some would say it is all down to box office success. Others would say that it's measured by entertainment value, special effects, A-list actors, original screenplays or critical acclaim. I believe cinematic greatness goes deeper than all these. The reason I chose the ten films in this book is because they had a significant effect on my life. Each one has been transformational in its own way, by *changing my thinking, challenging my behaviours* or *creating a different worldview.*

Following a stream of dreary movies in the seventies, the arrival of *Star Wars* would forever change people's cinema-going experiences. Just as *Jaws* caused beach attendance to plummet, and *Juno* challenged people's views on abortion, other movies began to challenge culture and change people's view of the world. One of these, at least, starred one of cinema's greatest acting talents, Robin Williams.

During his all too short acting career, Robin Williams won five Grammys, four Golden Globes, two Screen Actors Guild

---

6. James 4:14, KJV.

Awards, two Emmys, and an Oscar. While *Hook* (1991), *Mrs Doubtfire* (1993), *Good Will Hunting* (1997), *Patch Adams* (1998) and *August Rush* (2007) were good films, to me Williams scaled the heights of cinematic greatness in his portrayal of Mr. Keating in the film *Dead Poets Society.* Receiving rave reviews, *Dead Poets Society* is regarded by many as the most inspirational movie of all time. Offering a huge dose of the 'feel-good-factor', this was one of the must-go-to films of its time, and arguably the first multi-viewing movie of its day. Even those with a short memory admit that this movie has an enduring quality about it. Three decades on and it still has the power to inspire the viewer. With its unusual take on duty, honour, obligation, family, idealism, expectation, and life and death, *Dead Poets Society* seems as relevant today as when it first hit the cinema screens back in 1989.

This masterpiece strangely resonates with my childhood. While I was not a privileged American boy growing up in the 1950s, but rather a working-class British lad from the industrial heartland of the United Kingdom, this story has some clear similarities to my formative years.

Growing up in the 1950s, my childhood was something of a monochrome and monotone existence.

There were occasional breaks from this. One of my earliest memories is that of a heavily distorted electronic sound coming from an antique wood-veneered radio. In the era before television, the radio and the daily newspaper were our window onto the world. Carefully positioned in the corner of the backroom of our brick-built, end of terrace home in the suburbs of Coventry, this radio gave us programmes that became family favourites.

An example.

It's 6.45pm on a chilly winter evening. The whole family is huddled around a blazing coal fire. In a house that lacks any form of central heating, the fireplace is a focal point for the family. Tuned to BBC Radio 4, the crackling radio competes with the noise the roaring fire. Half a century on and it only takes a few bars of the famous theme tune to be transported back into these familiar surroundings. The only one missing from this homely huddle is Toby, a dog of questionable pedigree. Toby is a black and white terrier-like mutt and has been exiled to the coal shed. Accused of nipping the ankles of a passing cyclist who once rode down the narrow lane at the side of our house, Toby is more of a guard dog than a family pet.

With the evening meal finished and everything tidied away, it is time for another episode of the everyday life of country folk set in the fictional village of Ambridge. The world's longest soap opera has for us become the highlight of 1950s family entertainment. I am talking about *The Archers*. Jump forward a few years and the radio has been relegated to a secondary form of family entertainment, with pride of place given to a black and white television set with a ten-inch screen, manufactured by Bush Ltd. In reality, this freestanding piece of furniture could hardly be called black and white. In terms of picture quality, it was grey, drizzled with electrical interference. And back then, the BBC (British Broadcasting Corporation) offered only one channel. Programmes ran from three in the afternoon till eleven thirty at night. Closure was marked by the sound of the British National Anthem. This was accompanied on the television by a disappearing test card that would eventually be reduced to a single white disappearing dot in the middle of the screen.

Looking back, it is difficult to see how the fifties was viewed as the golden age of children's television when the highlight of my week was an episode of *Davey Crockett, King of the New Frontier*. As if my childhood was not bland enough, any photographic evidence of my existence is recorded in the form of small, square, poorly focused black and white photographs. Captured on my parent's Brownie Kodak box camera, these have been reduced to a pile of old crumpled, greyish photographs.

How then does *Dead Poets Society* resonate with my childhood, and to the extent that it takes the number one position in this book? The answer is found in the two characters, John Keating and Todd Anderson. In the first, I see a creative teaching gift for which I aspire. In the second, I see a character with whom I closely associate and identify.

Set in the fictional elite Vermont boarding school known as Welton Academy, we meet Robin Williams' character, Mr Keating. As a former graduate turned English teacher, he strikes up a unique relationship with some young men by daring them to address him as, "O Captain, my Captain." Breaking with tradition, Keating attempts to portray poetry as an essential part of everyday life, rather than a boring part of the school's core curriculum. He urges them to stand on their desks, rip pages out of textbooks and develop their own way of walking.

No one who has watched this movie can forget the opening scene. Taking his students from the classroom to the school lobby, Keating encourages them to study the trophies and photos of former graduates, getting them to consider the brevity of life. In stating, "We're all food for worms," he teaches that life is but a fleeting moment and those who 'seize the day' and 'make the most of time' can live extraordinary lives. Of course, none of this goes unnoticed. Keating's bizarre methods quickly come to the attention of headmaster Nolan.

For years Welton has churned out the stereotypical graduate, but now they are being challenged to think outside the well-worn tracks of previous generations. Although initially suspicious of his methodology, some students are inspired to embrace the change both inside and outside the classroom. A few students even attempt to resurrect the somewhat secretive gatherings known as the *Dead Poets Society*.

Shy Guy

The parental pressure on the students in this story is immense, pushing them to the brink. Neil Perry's father tells him that he and his mother are expecting great things from him. This heavy weight of great expectations is increased when headmaster Nolan welcomes Todd Anderson to the school, telling him that he has big shoes to fill, and reminding him that his brother was one of the school's finest students. When it comes to parental pressure I can to a much lesser degree empathise with Neil Perry and Todd Anderson. Like them, my early life was lived under the shadow of my father's expectations. Although he never said, "We expect great things from you," it was inferred in so many other ways.

Making numerous sacrifices to build a successful hardware store, my father fully intended that his two sons would inherit the business. The weight of duty and obligation this caused was a very heavy burden. My older brother fulfilled my father's dream. I was the one who dared to disappoint. Like Perry and Anderson, I slowly began to emerge from the shadows of my father's expectations and plot my own journey through life. Don't get me wrong. I had two wonderful parents who sacrificed time, energy and resources to give my brother and me a great start in life. But the expectation to work in the business after school and at weekends created a loathing that culminated in a desire to have nothing to do with it. Although his motives were honourable, my father's unspoken expectations would eventually force me to make a choice that would have far reaching financial implications whose shockwaves still reverberate today.

Perhaps this is the reason I resonate with Todd Anderson, played by Ethan Hawke, who is portrayed as a shy guy who stammers and is not great at socialising with his fellow students. As an introverted, nervous student who hates public speaking, his first attempt at poetry in his poem, 'Not Good Enough', is a perfect expression of his personal struggles. Preferring to stay in the shadows, Todd is the total opposite of his gregarious, outgoing, would-be actor of a roommate, Neil Perry, played by Robert Sean. Unable to share his concerns with his parents, the faculty or his roommate, Mr. Keating encourages Todd to stand up for himself and discover his inner voice through poetry.

In so many ways, Todd's search for significance is my journey.

Those character traits of shyness, non-socialising, nervousness, feelings of 'not being good enough' and preferring the shadows to the limelight – well, that's me. Uncomfortable in my own skin, I developed the ability to play the part.

John Powell wrote a book called *Why Am I Afraid to Tell You Who I Really Am?*[7] Using his categories, I played games and fulfilled the roles of:

'Mr. Always Right'
'The Clown'
'The Conformist'
'The Cynic'
'The Dominator'
'The Fragile Handle with Care'
'The Loner'
'The Martyr'
'The Strong Silent Type'.

I played them all to perfection. Hoping to find acceptance, approval and appreciation, I projected an image I believed would garner the applause of others. But I was living an unrealistic fantasy rather than a realised dream.

I was in desperate need of a Keating-type person, a true investor who would challenge my thinking so that I might change my behaviour. I can thankfully say that there were and have always been investors who did just that – men and women who have instructed me in the redemptive process of ripping out some of the pages from my past that sought to define me. These people have encouraged me to stand on desks to find a different perspective on life. Teachers, pastors, friends, work colleagues, preachers, parents, authors and a loving partner, all have helped me find my inner voice so that I can stand up and be counted. To those people I say, "Thank you."

My Barbaric Yawp

Silence is the atmosphere in which the introverted do business. To speak or say too much is to risk being caught out as a fraud.

---

7. John Powell, *Why Am I Afraid to Tell You Who I Really Am?*, Argus Communications, 1969.

Remaining silent in a crowd, with the occasional nod of the head in agreement with the speaker, can make you look profound, even when you have little idea what is being discussed.

Todd Anderson was a shy guy struggling to find his voice. It takes the extreme methods of his teacher and the death of his roommate for him to finally stand up and be counted. With the influence of one and the impact of the other, eventually Todd discovers what the poet Walt Whitman called "my barbaric yawp"[8] – a loud cry or yell that comes from deep within a person.

Like Todd, I grew up with a sense of self-loathing. Full of self-doubt and a deep sense of inadequacy, I never felt that I measured up. Outwardly I put on a great act, but inwardly I felt vulnerable and battled against a deep sense of unworthiness. My overwhelming self-belief was that I was not clever enough, cool enough, or strong enough to offer any significant contribution to the world around me. Most of the time, I had this inner drive to run away and hide – strange when you consider that much of my life from my early twenties has involved public speaking. The mere mention of my name in a public setting would send shivers down my spine and cause my face to redden. Like the biblical character King Saul, my physical stature may have me "head and shoulders above the crowd",[9] but take it from me, tallness is not all it's cracked up to be. As with King Saul, when I was picked out from the crowd, I would be filled with a deep desire to run. The opportunity to fulfil my God-given destiny was being thwarted by low self-esteem and a poor self-image.

I am by nature a reluctant leader, someone who still gets nervous when given the opportunity to speak publicly. Whether its tens, hundreds or thousands of listeners, before stepping onto a platform I have to silence the voices in my head

---

8. Walt Whitman, *Song of Myself*, 1892.
9. 1 Samuel 9:2, MSG.

that attempt to question my God-given calling as a preacher and teacher.

We are all a product of our past, and despite those people, objects or events that would silence us, we all need to find our voice, our barbaric yawp.

The world does not need more *echoes* that merely repeat what others are saying; it needs prophetic *voices* crying in the wilderness of social need and spiritual ignorance. It needs those who will take their stand on the stage of history and become a modern version of John the Baptist, people whose demeanour demonstrates their total dependence on God and who proclaim truth, pointing the way for others to follow. John Keating, Welton's charismatic English teacher, tells each of the boys to find their own voice and to do it quickly. The longer they wait to start this process, the less likely they will be to discover their voice and use it. If the real me is what I think, love, hate, feel, value, honour, esteem, desire, hope for, believe in and am committed to,[10] then few people know the person behind the public persona.

The real 'you' is who you are when you are all alone.

It becomes so easy to put on an act, to play a part and project an image that is far removed from who you are. When this happens, we rob the world of what my old professor would call, 'The Uniqueness of Otherness', or what the New Testament terms "the multicoloured grace of God".[11]

When we refuse to be true to ourselves, we rob society of our colourful character and we do little to change what we might

---

10. Why Am I Afraid to Tell You Who I Really Am, p.8.
11. 1 Peter 4:10 paraphrased – The word translated 'varied' means 'many coloured'.

see as bland and boring. As a shy guy, I struggle to conquer those perfectionist tendencies that make me fear getting things wrong. Internalising so much, it would take the Mr Keatings of this world to help me find my "barbaric yawp". Keating's radical approach to poetry was as revolutionary as it was refreshing. He didn't merely get his pupils to think outside the box; he had them destroy the box altogether.

The Keating Effect

Bill Clinton, Muhammad Ali, Whoopi Goldberg, Stan Smith, Colin Powell and Danny Glover all have something in common. They have all experienced 'The Keating Effect'.

Bill Clinton experienced it through his grandfather and great uncle Buddy who in his early childhood became the dominant male influence on his life. Uncle Buddy taught Billy to appreciate all kinds of people and to listen to what they say. He taught him the importance of respect and resilience.

When pushed to name the one major influence in his life, Muhammad Ali named Nelson Mandela. He became "a symbol of what it means to sacrifice one's life for a cause as great as freedom",[12] of the man who seeks to fight for something greater than himself.

For Whoopi Goldberg it was her mum who taught her to value true friendship and those on the outside of the in-group. She taught Whoopi to be sure to make them feel good about themselves, no matter what. And when you mess up, to take responsibility for your actions and apologise.

Retired Tennis star Stan Smith found that his coach would not only teach him tennis but, as a father figure, would teach him table manners. His coach not only taught him to handle a racket, but how to hold a knife and fork.

---

12. Denzel Washington, A Hand to Guide Me, Meredith Books, 2006, p.29.

Gen. Colin L. Powell, USA (retired) puts his success down to a group of people. Growing up with a network of aunts, uncles and cousins, Powell places great emphasis on the fact that it 'takes a tribe' to bring up a child.

The Actor Danny Glover points to his third-grade teacher, someone who, before young people could be diagnosed as dyslexic, saw that Danny was struggling with words but loved numbers. She encouraged him to take ownership of what he was good at to feel a growing sense of self-worth.

The common denominator in all these people is the fact that they all experienced 'The Keating Effect'.

Finding Keating

True transformation cannot happen in isolation. We all need investors who will lovingly challenge our beliefs as well as our behaviour, individuals who will build a strong relational bridge before stepping in to break up our comfort zone, rattle our cage and tip us out of the nest. Their actions might shake us to the core, but their goal is to bring the best out of us. Although their words and actions might disturb us, eventually they should inspire us to go further than we've ever gone before.

Whether they are with close friends or casual acquaintances, these relational encounters are based on mutual trust that will, over time, result in radical transformation. While some Keatings we might meet face-to-face, others we will know only through books, or through one of the many forms of electronic communication available to us.

Some of these encounters may be fleeting while others may be long lasting; some investors will be living, while others may have passed away. The *who, what, where* or *when* is not important; the important thing is to let people step into our learning circle and enable us to revolutionise our sphere of influence.

The great influencers in my life have changed my perceptions, challenged my behaviour, opened doors of opportunity, modelled a different way of doing life, and enabled me to live the immediate in the light of the ultimate. They have taken me out of myself and pushed me beyond my limited perceptions. Preachers, teachers, musicians, work colleagues, authors and actors – the list is almost endless – they have all orchestrated a melody that has caused me to 'seize the day', to 'make the most of time', and helped to find my "barbaric yarp". Whether they are mentors, coaches or disciplers, they all serve to bring about 'The Keating Effect'. Coming alongside to journey with us, they see our latent potential and are willing to invest time, energy and resources to bring about exponential growth. This is the greenhouse effect that fast tracks our growth and readies us to be planted in a new environment. Given the right amount of care, the greenhouse effect will cause the seed to germinate and grow into its full potential.

In the closing scene of *Dead Poets Society,* it is the shy, nervous, introverted Todd Anderson who leads a class rebellion against the old school ways of headmaster Nolan. Todd is the first to stand on his desk and shout, "O Captain, my Captain." Honouring the contribution that the now disgraced Mr. Keating has made in his life, Todd speaks, and others follow. Refusing to let his restrictive past censor his present reality, Mr Anderson truly 'seizes the day'!

Parachute Packers

In the search for significance we all want to 'make our lives extraordinary'. And while some might interpret significance as fame and fortune, or becoming the focus of attention, true significance is *being the best you can be with the skills you have, no matter what environment you find yourself in.*

Sitting in a Kansas City restaurant, a retired USA Airforce pilot was approached by a total stranger. Seated two tables away, the stranger had for some time been staring at the former pilot; that is until his intuition got the better of him. Standing up, he walked over to the table and introduced himself.

"You're Captain Plump," he announced.

Somewhat startled the officer replied, "Yes sir, I am."

"You flew jet fighters in Vietnam," the stranger continued. "You were on the aircraft carrier Kitty Hawk. You were shot down. You parachuted into enemy hands and spent six years as a prisoner of war."

"How in the world did you know all that?"

"Because I packed your parachute," the stranger said.

With that, a shocked Lt. General Stuart Beare (aka Captain Plump) stood to his feet and proffered his hand and his thanks.

"I guess it worked, then," the parachute packer said.

"Yes sir, indeed it did. And I must tell you, I've said a lot of prayers of thanks for your nimble fingers, but I never thought I'd have the opportunity to express my gratitude in person."[13]

The parachute packers on the Kitty Hawk worked in the bowels of the carrier, rarely seeing daylight, working in humid conditions.

Unseen, unknown and unnamed, these individuals laboured behind the scenes to make sure that if the worst happened, pilots would have the wherewithal to survive.

Who, then, is your parachute packer? Who is working behind the scenes to make sure you survive when tragedy strikes?

Maybe we should turn that question on its head, "Are you willing to pack parachutes, to work behind the scenes to secure the success of others?"

---

13. The Parachute Packer – the Best Story I have Heard, Forbes Magazine, July 18 2012.

We might never become an 'A-listed' personality but being the best version of 'you' is all God asks. We might be called to play second fiddle, to take up a supportive role to some superstar. But if being the best version of you involves being in the bowels of an organisation – a relative unknown fulfilling a supportive role – then fulfil your destiny in a way that would make your heavenly father happy. Becoming an understudy might be exactly what is required for you to live an extraordinary life.

The business magnate Sir Richard Branson recently listed fifteen influences that operated 'The Keating Effect' on his life. The person top of his list might not be the person you were expecting: "More than anyone else, my mum taught me the value of hard work, independence and an entrepreneurial spirit – and year after year she continues to serve as a great mentor in my life and in business . . . Mum has always been my biggest inspiration as a person, let alone as an entrepreneur."[14]

Captain, my Captain

If the quality of a movie were to be measured by its ability to move us emotionally, then *Dead Poets Society* would score high, the final frames being true tear-jerkers.

Unfairly and unceremoniously fired from his teaching position, Mr Keating readies himself to exit the classroom one final time. As he does, his ardent followers consider how to honour his passing. Faced with the prospect of headmaster Nolan now teaching Keating's poetry class, those impacted by 'The Keating Effect' stand on their desks. One by one they each begin to declare their allegiance to the departing teacher in classic Keating style, "O Captain, my Captain." Mr Keating leaves saying a double thank you to his boys.

---

14. http://www.slice.ca/money/photos/sir-richard-branson-reveals-the-people-who-inspire-him-most/#!A-Branson-Getty-455045518-resized.

I will be forever grateful to those individuals who brought about 'The Keating Effect' in my life.

To those who saw potential when others didn't, who challenged my small-mindedness, ignored my insecurity and encouraged me to rip out the pages that other people had written about me. To those who helped me find my "barbaric yawp", to see life from a different perspective, to step outside the confines of previous generations, to think innovatively, to push me out of the nest and fly.

To you all, I stand on the desk of my life and, looking towards a new horizon, say a double thank you too.

KEEPING IT REEL

Mistakes I Have Made:

- Taking too long to find my voice.
- Failing to rip out the pages from my past.
- Cowering beneath authority figures.
- Living according to the expectations of others.
- Letting the family of fear, stress and anxiety take up residence.

Lessons I Have Learnt:

- Life is short.
- Don't overstay your welcome.
- Instructors are plentiful, but investors are few.
- Leave a legacy that causes others to stand on their desk.
- Always have an exit strategy.

CHAPTER

TRAILER

Chariots of Fire (1981) – winner of four Oscars – is a fact-based film produced by Lord David Puttnam. The story focuses on two athletes competing at the 1924 Olympic Games. The first, Eric Liddell, is the protagonist or hero of the film. A strong and principled Christian, Liddell refuses to run on Sundays, believing that he would thereby break one of the ten commandments. Harold Abrahams, an English Jew, is running to overcome people's racial stereotypes and prejudices. While Abrahams eventually wins the 100 metres Gold, Liddell, when he discovers that his 100 metres race is to take place on a Sunday, refuses to compete. A friend of his then generously gives Liddell his place in the 400 metres. Against all odds, Liddell wins the Gold. At the end, we are told that Abrahams became the elder statesman of British athletics, while Liddell lived out his days as a missionary in China, and all of Scotland mourned his death in 1945. In this chapter, we look at how a sense of divine calling can produce an unstoppable passion in your life, leading you to make a stand for God where necessary, and in the end to finish well. When we run God's race for our lives (as opposed to our own), we truly feel His divine pleasure.

PEOPLE WITH PASSION

Chariots of Fire

Most movie fans would only need to hear the opening bars of Vangelis' musical score to recognise our next movie – six notes played on an electronic keyboard would probably be enough. If we then added a screenshot of barefoot athletes running along a deserted, sandy beach in 1920s sports gear, the clues would be complete. We're talking about the Hollywood blockbuster, *Chariots of Fire*.

Chariots of Fire seemed to set the scene for the entrepreneurial eighties. The so-called Decade of Decadence was a time when anything seemed possible and, for those in the right place at the right time, it was. *Chariots of Fire* seemed to capture some of the hopes and aspirations of the viewing public. With its award-winning screenplay and musical score, this was one of the must-watch movies of its day.

Yet *Chariots of Fire* is far more than the sum of its mesmerising music and inspiring acting. This is a movie full of learning moments.

Although athletics is an unfamiliar world to me personally and therefore outside my comfort zone, the film is a great hook on which to hang some life lessons from my past.

Milk Race

Confession, they say, is good for the soul. If that is right, then the next few sentences are going to improve my mental health no end.

When it comes to sporting experience and expertise, my life is woefully short. Having traced my family history back to the 1700s, it seems as if someone chlorinated the gene pool – making the 'athletics gene' notable by its absence. With neither the passion nor the physique, I spent my school years trying to excuse myself from all sporting activity. In high school, my Physical Education teachers thought it best to insist that an overweight, tall teenager (that's me!) should enrol in such things as boxing, rugby, javelin throwing, shot putting and cross country running. Whether on the field or in the gym, the two years I spent trying – but never succeeding – to springboard over the confounded, leather-bound wooden vaulting box highlighted my lack of sporting ability. Had I been brave enough, and the teacher less likely to blow a fuse, I would have pointed people to the ancient writings of the Apostle Paul, specifically to his statement that "bodily exercise profiteth little".[15] My achievements?

I was a fearful captain of the school rugby team, a disqualified shot putter, and I won my one and only boxing match because no one could be found to equal my heavy weight status.

My sole success, although short lived, was to achieve an unexpected third place in a high school cross country race. The surprised look on my games master's face was worth all the effort and ingenuity. However, my bronze award was short lived; a more deserving prize-winner reported me for cheating.

Running unsupervised through the English countryside, I fell further and further behind until I saw a passing milk cart. Although only battery-powered, sitting on the platform with a load of rattling milk crates seemed to me a better way to travel. This was to me an inspired act of ingenuity but perhaps waving at my fellow competitors as I passed them by was not the best idea, although it certainly made me feel good. A few yards from the finish, I jumped off my borrowed transport and ran across the line, ending up third in my whole school year.

---

15. 1 Timothy 4:8 KJV.

Hardly *Chariots of Fire*!

But this doesn't mean the film isn't important to me. It may not have any relevance athletically, but it does vocationally. My athletic failures should therefore in no way underestimate the numerous learning moments from *Chariots of Fire*. Based around the 1924 Olympics, this movie is an exploration of how *passion* and *purpose* are born out of *calling*. We can see this in the stories of Eric Liddell, a devout Scottish Christian, and Harold Abrahams, an English Jew. And it's something I can see in my life too, to a lesser degree.

Tsunami of the Soul

Chariots of Fire celebrates the driving force behind two young men from different backgrounds, individuals who wanted to become the fastest athletes of their day.

Having discovered what they were good at, their overwhelming passion pushed them to perfect their athletic ability. Each in their own way had found a purpose bigger than themselves, that special something that gave them clarity of thought and singleness of vision. This was no momentary fad or passing fancy; this was a force to be reckoned with, an all-consuming zeal that turned obstacles into opportunities, swept perceived limitations aside and cleared the way for personal success. This was a *tsunami of the soul.*

If I could talk to each of my grandchildren as they considered their future career, I would encourage them to find the one thing they are good at and to stop caring what other people think about them, not to allow peers, parents, teachers or culture dictate their direction. I would challenge them to find, feed and follow their passion, because passionate people do incredible things. I would urge them to avoid becoming casual consumers of the temporal and to be consumed by the eternal. Like Jesus, I would love my grandchildren to be thoroughly overwhelmed with the purpose of God.[16]

Like Father like Son, Jesus lived in a continual state of enthusiasm.

Consumed with a godly passion, Jesus demonstrated a zeal for life that was made up of a 'passionate commitment', 'motivating force', 'raging fire', 'fighting spirit' and 'Godlike enthusiasm'.[17] I'd want my grandchildren to know this level of Christ-like passion that says, "If I'm not making someone else's life better, then they are wasting my own."

With a commitment to his Father's will, Jesus had a compassion for others and a willingness to be inconvenienced. His compulsion to fulfil heaven's will on earth demonstrated the true essence of the *tsunami of the soul* – a godly passion that swept away self-centeredness, doubts and fears and left in its wake a radically changed environment. It's this driving force that gets you up in the morning, that keeps you awake

---

16. John 2:17, Psalms 69:9; 119:139.
17. 17 The word translated 'zeal' – zelos, see Romans 10:2; 2 Corinthians 7:7–11; 9:2; Philippians 3:6.

at night and motivates you to break through all perceived limitations and, when necessary, take God-inspired risks.

George Lucas, the highly respected filmmaker once said, "You have to find something that you love enough to be able to take risks, jump over the hurdles and break through the brick walls that are always going to be placed in front of you. If you don't have that kind of feeling for what it is you are doing, you'll stop at the first hurdle."[18]

In a Western civilisation, in which a false view of tolerance and compromise has created a version of Christianity that is a bland imitation of what God intended, the world needs passionate people to make the difference, spiritual athletes driven by a passion and purpose that flows from a deep, immoveable sense of call.

God Came Calling

I grew up listening to preachers telling me about the importance of 'finding your calling'. I have also spoken about this principle. Sadly, it is wrong! It is based on the idea that it is we who take the initiative, we who do the finding. While there is an element of truth in this, the Bible shows that men like Samuel never tried to find their calling; their calling found them. Perhaps the greatest of the Old Testament prophets, Samuel was a class act; he served a nation that was falling apart at the seams. Yet because of his willingness to serve the purpose of God in obscurity, God came calling with a phenomenal opportunity.

Looking back over my God-given "three score years and ten",[19] those looking in from the outside might ask the following questions.

---

18. Battle Cries for the Hollywood Underdog: Motivation & Inspiration for Your Journey to the Top, by Monroe Mann, Lou Bortone. 2013, Battle Cry 60.
19. Psalm 90:10.

"Why do you do what you do?"

"Why did you refuse the easy option of working for your natural father?"

"Why have you lived in fourteen different properties, resided on two different continents, travelled through Europe, North and South America, Africa and Canada?"

"Why have you been involved in five different streams of Christianity in the UK?"

I can only give one answer to this list of questions. It is because of the passion that I've felt in my heart – a passion that arises out of my sense of calling. And that's why *Chariots of Fire* is such a seminal movie for me. In Eric Liddell, we see a man with an unquenchable passion. That passion is expressed in his extraordinary dedication to his sport – the long amounts of time and energy spent in being the best he could possibly be. But this passion was not something that existed on its own. No, it flowed out of Liddell's sense of calling. There it is: *passion, purpose* and *calling*.

Back in the mid-nineties, while studying church leadership in Portland, Oregon, I was set an assignment to write a short piece of work entitled: 'My Awareness of Calling'. My answer, although somewhat religious in its wording and dated in its style, outlines what happened to me when God came calling:

Growing up in a godly environment, I fostered from an early age a desire to serve God, yet this was often overshadowed by feelings of personal inadequacy. Through prayer, godly direction and practical discipline, the Holy Spirit prepared me for service and began to "nullify the things that are, so that no one should boast before [God]".[20] Once ignited, that inner sense of purpose, although not crystallised in all its aspects, began to burn with greater intensity.

---

20. 1 Corinthians 1:28–29.

It's thirty years later now and that drive to take others by the hand and lead them in their God-given destiny still constrains me; that longing to take the bread of life and, with God's blessing, break it in into bite-sized pieces to feed the hungry, still consumes me; that passion to mine the gold of revelatory truth from the rock of God's Word, craft it through study and research, then have the eternal assayer place His stamp of anointing on it, still crowns my every desire and goal in life. Just as the wind causes a sailboat to cut a swathe through strong waves, so the sense of divine call drives me ever onward "to take hold of that for which Christ Jesus took hold of me".[21]

It is this call, this sense of purpose, that gets me up in the morning, that motivates me when others conspire to derail me.

It's this call that causes me to accept the inconvenience that a commitment to the will of God involves and to trust in the goodness of God to provide all I need, to draw on the grace of God to do what in my own strength I cannot do – to lean on the mercy of God when I've messed up, to endure the spiritual abuse of others, to spend time, energy and limited resources on investing in numerous relocations. All of this is because in New Testament terms we discovered years ago "the treasure hidden in the field" and sacrificed all we had to purchase the field.[22]

For or Against

Passion without purpose is a waste and leads to frustration, but passion born out of purpose is the secret of a fulfilled life. Eric

---

21. Philippians 3:12.
22. Matthew 13:44, NASB.

Liddell exemplifies this in *Chariots of Fire*. He was prepared to endure any number of tests. He was uncompromisingly single-minded. He would not bow down to peer pressure in his determination to finish well.[23] Fulfilling God's calling was the be-all and end-all of his life.

It is interesting to note here that although Abrahams and Liddell were potential Olympic competitors, they are both depicted as running for different reasons. While Abrahams runs *against* the pressure and prejudice of others, Liddell runs with passion and purpose *for* a well-defined cause. We might put it this way: Abrahams embraced a *reactionary* mindset, Liddell a *responsive* mindset.

These two philosophies showcase some of the problems in modern Christianity. All too often, Christians adopt the Abrahams approach. We become adversarial activists who have an isolationist approach to the world. Creating a ghetto mentality, we critique the present culture rather than create an alternative one. If we insist on running our race this way, the Church will continue its decline towards irrelevancy.

As individuals we are not called to *compete* with society, but to understand our reason for being and *complete* the course set out before us.

As Christ-followers, our approach to culture must surely be more like Eric Liddell's. He was inspired by a divine calling. Both before and after the human applause dissipated, his was a responsive rather than a reactionary approach to the world

---

23. The journalist Andrew Pulver, describing Eric Liddell's performance in this film, writes that 'a deeply believing Christian refused to kowtow to slimy crypto-fascist Edward VIII to be.' Film Blog, 'I can see why Gordon Brown likes Chariots of Fire, The Guardian, 11 May 2009.

around him. He created culture more than he challenged culture. He was responsive more than reactionary. His goal was to complete more than to compete.

What about you?

Has your philosophy been reactionary (*against*) or responsive (*for*)?

Looking back at the way I have run my race, I see more Abrahams than Liddell in my approach to people, objects and events. Mine has often been a more reactionary than responsive approach. Like Abrahams, I was driven by the pressure and prejudice of others instead of the passion and purpose that fuelled Liddell to do what he did.

Our tent leaves a dent. Wherever we reside in this life, we knowingly or unknowingly leave a lasting impression on the environment, something that says, "I was here!" Sadly, in my case, all too often I have not left a positive impression.

In the recent stage play based on *Chariots of Fire*, Abrahams says this, commenting on Liddell's running: "I was faster," but "Eric was better."[24] Abrahams was not talking about Liddell's sprinting technique here; he thought it 'laboured'. Rather, he was referring to his deeply held principles as a committed Christian. In all that Liddell said and did in life, whether in competitive sport or on the mission field in China, he left a lasting impression. He was known for what he was for, not what he was against. He didn't try to compete with those around him; his single-minded focus was on completing the call of God on his life. There was no separation of spiritual and secular activities in Liddell's life; everything he did was for the glory of God.

---

24. "What Happened to the Chariots of Fire Heroes?" Julie Carpenter, *Express Newspaper*, Thursday May 24, 2012.

Reason for Being

Chariots of Fire is for me is a film that evokes that most pressing of questions: "Why do I do what I do?" The answer to this is what gets us out of bed in the morning. It is what motivates us to go the second mile, to love the unlovable, to be present when others are absent, to serve without any thought of reward, to give without a thought of receiving, to lay our lives down for the greater good. To lose this divine imperative is to run the risk of becoming an also-ran. With a passion to fulfil God's purpose for our lives, we run for a cause far greater than ourselves.

In our all-too-human search for significance, we look everywhere except God's perfect will. Eric Liddell believed in a divine purpose for his life and a measure of grace to fulfil it. We see this in the most memorable quote of the whole movie. When explaining his actions to his misunderstanding sister Jenny, Liddell tells her that he believes God made him for a purpose, and that God made him to run fast. When he runs, he feels God's pleasure

We all have the capability to engage in meaningful activity, be it paid or non-paid, full-time, part-time or volunteering. Coming as it did at the dawn of the Decade of Decadence, this film carried a prophetic warning to the Western world, that behind all our striving for more, our goal must be more than simply the applause of others. Human beings are created to need a purpose greater than position, pay packet or promotion. If it lies in those things, then we are likely to end our race uncertain if we won or lost and ask, "What was all that about?"

My wife Tina tells a story from her own childhood. While stationed at a Royal Air Force base, her father, a serving officer, entered her into the sports day. The race she remembers is the one she won. Her father was standing proudly at the finishing line. He carried her around in his arms, boasting to family and friends of her win. Tina, however, was more concerned about her prize – a bar of chocolate – and standing on the podium to enjoy the applause of others.

In all we say and do in life, whether we win or lose in God's eyes, we are "winners who sometimes lose, not losers who sometimes win".

So, forget the prize, stop looking for the podium, and enjoy the Father's loving embracing as he lifts you high and says, "Well done, good and faithful servant." This is what Eric Liddell teaches us. He did not run to *earn* God's pleasure; he did what he was good at doing and, as a child of God, he knew instinctively that whatever he did to serve the purpose of God in the earth, it would bring a smile to his heavenly father's face. His was not an act of servitude born out a legalistic view of God. Rather, he revelled in his sonship – a position of divine favour not dependent on human performance. Like Jesus, whom Liddell wholeheartedly followed, he sensed heaven's applause:

"This is my beloved son, in whom I am well pleased."[25]

Whether we are parents doing the 3am shift, carers of an elderly relative, an unappreciated employee, overworked manager, unrecognised volunteer, we should not run for the applause of others but because we know that our heavenly father stands at the finishing line ready to sweep you off our feet and show us off in heaven.

Don't be driven by profit, pressure, performance or unrealised expectations.

Run for the glory of God.

Don't compete against others in your life. Concentrate on completing your own race. Stepping outside your prescribed

---

25. Matthew 3:17, ESV.

lane, you run the risk of being discouraged and even disqualified[26] – something the Apostle Paul and the Book of Proverbs warn us about.[27]

Culture Creators

Don't think that your calling is necessarily going to be outworked in an obviously Christian context. Yes, Eric Liddell ended up as a Christian missionary, but he began as an Olympic runner and served God's calling in his running as much as he did in his preaching. Maybe your calling is to represent Christ in the world of athletics. Maybe it's in the performing arts or in the academic arena. Maybe it's in a more practical activity such as plumbing, carpentry, bricklaying or electrical work. Whatever God gives us to do, we should do it with all our heart. For that to happen, we will need to find an ultimate purpose for why we do what we do.

In the book *Peak Performers,* we are told that when NASA wanted to put a man on the moon, every individual displayed a high level of drive and enthusiasm. Motivation was an integral part of their working lives. However, once the moon landing had been achieved, people became lethargic.

Once God's calling finds us, we must keep our drive alive. We must not replicate the Man on the Moon scenario. We must keep our focus and that focus is not on *critiquing* our culture but in *creating* a new culture, a culture that reflects the values of the Kingdom of Heaven here on earth.

That, in many ways, is the challenge we Christians face today. We can either be reactionaries or revolutionaries. Reactionaries fight against culture. Revolutionaries work towards creating a new culture. While Abrahams set out to *challenge the culture,*

---

26. 2 Corinthians 10:12-18; 1 Corinthians 9:27; Proverbs 29:18.
27. Proverbs 29:18, literal translation of the word 'unrestrained', NASB.

Liddell determined by God's grace to *create a different culture.* And although the two might sound the same, there is a big difference between them. For Eric Liddell, being *responsive* rather than *reactionary* meant understanding that Jesus Christ came to create a counterculture, an alternative community, known as the Kingdom of Heaven. His focus was therefore not about competing with the present culture, or critiquing it, or even changing it. His focus was on creating an entirely new culture, heaven on earth.

Too many Christians today seek to impose moral standards on people who believe in entirely different philosophies and worldviews. They seek to legislate morality, to pass and impose Christian laws on non-Christian people. This merely produces a facade of Christianity; underneath, nothing has changed. Prohibition is a classic example. Making alcohol illegal only drove drinking underground.

If we define culture as 'the way we do things around here', then those who make a lasting difference do so by being the change rather than merely calling for change. Whether in the home, community or workplace, our call as Christ-followers is to live by example, to create in word and deed the kind of culture that reflects Christian values.

Less preaching and more practice would do our cause good!

None of this is to say it will be easy. Even Eric Liddell had his fair share of opposition. Both his family and his future King gave him a hard time, as did the Athletic Governing Board. However, in the face of all opposing factors, Liddell pushed through to gain the prize. Indeed, he was inflexible on that score.

In the New Testament, Christ-followers are explicitly told, "Don't let the world squeeze you into its mould." To be squeezed we first must become pliable. Maybe that's our problem as Christians today. Trying to be all things to all men, to fit in with the crowd, to be one of the boys, we become flexible on absolutes; we make God's truth more pliable to suit an ever-changing world.

Liddell was not a reactionary because he was secure in what he believed to be true. His responses came from a core belief in God's absolute truth. And this man was not for moving. And we shouldn't be either.

For Eric Liddell, there was to be no compromise.

When the Applause Ends

Speaking about *Chariots of Fire*, biographer Sally Magnusson reckoned that the real story of Abraham and Liddell occurs after the film's storyline has ended. Julie Carpenter, in an article for the *Express*, wrote this: "One Olympian died in a Japanese POW camp, the other was victim to a bizarre obsession."

Although history will record Eric Liddell as one of Scotland's greatest all-time sporting legends, his greatest achievement is seen in the story after the story. The Paris Olympics made him a superstar, but his years of missionary service in China made him one of Christianity's super-servants. Leaving the Olympic cheers behind, Eric – along with his father and brother – was posted to China by the London Missionary Service, where he died in a Prison of War camp. Exhibiting a truly altruistic attitude to the end, Liddell gave up the chance of freedom in a prisoner exchange by giving his place to a pregnant woman.[28]

---

28. "What Happened to the Chariots of Fire Heroes?" Julie Carpenter, *Express Newspaper*, Thursday May 24, 2012.

In Abrahams' life, the story after the story was altogether different. While the film depicted him as a man running from the anti-Semitic attitudes of the time, others see him as a man needing to out-perform his high-achieving brothers. His older brother had competed in the 1908 and 1912 Olympic Games. Abraham struggled with obsessive behaviour and other psychological problems. In his book *Running with Fire*, Mark Ryan, Abrahams' biographer, says, "His whole athletic life hinged on times." That obsession with time is seen in the fact that he carried two stopwatches with him everywhere and he timed everything. Abraham's pressure to perform may even have been rooted in pushy parents, for whom sporting achievement seemed everything.

Whatever the root cause, after the applause died down, Abrahams' search for significance was personally painful. Being defined by one race, he felt that the nation had forgotten his other athletic achievements. Abrahams' story after the story is a warning to us all. It's not how we start our race; it's how we end it that marks the *finishers* out from the *also-rans*.

Finishing Well

In life's journey, we should always keep the destination in view. For those who are nearer the end of the race, finishing well is an ever-present reality. Like the Apostle Paul, we all want to say, "This is the only race worth running. I've run hard right to the finish, believed all the way. All that's left now is the shouting – God's applause!"[29] This is what might be termed *living your immediate in the light of an ultimate*. Life is not a 100m dash based on speed, it is a marathon that takes skill, stamina and persistence to complete. In this long race, we are not competing against others, but rather completing our individual race. The

---

29. 2 Timothy 4:6-8, MSG.

time it takes could be longer for one than for another, but it is reaching the finishing line that really matters.

One way or another, we will all finish our race. The question is, how will we finish?

It is reckoned that the Bible mentions around a thousand leaders. Of one hundred leaders or so, we have enough data to make a judgement on how they finished. There were those who were taken out of the game through poor behaviour, those who finished badly, those who finished without reaching their full potential, and finally those who clearly finished well. The last group are in the minority.[30]

If we are going to be real, or 'reel', we need to admit that we are a strange mixture of failure and success, weakness and strength, in this respect. The Old Testament prophet Elijah is a perfect example. I mention him specifically because he is taken up to heaven at the end of his life in a *chariot of fire*. As complex characters go, there is perhaps none more so than Elijah, and yet it is this very complexity that makes him not only very human but also very relatable.

In one season of his life, Elijah seemed to display both the strengths and weakness of Liddell and Abrahams. In 1 Kings 18, we find him running under "the hand of God"[31] – which is reminiscent of Liddell running for God's pleasure. In the very next chapter, we find him changing into an Abrahams-type personality as he now runs from the prejudicial threats of a woman named Jezebel.

---

30. Dr. J. Robert Clinton, "Finishing Well. The Challenge of a Lifetime." Copyright 1994, Barnabas Publishers.
31. 1 Kings 18:46, NASB.

Perhaps this mixture resides in most of us. One minute we are running *for* our passion and purpose in life, feeling God's pleasure in the process. The next, we are running *from* such things as our past, our fears, our inconsistencies, insecurities and low self-esteem. We might even find ourselves running from the threats or prejudices of other people, as Elijah did. All this seems to have happened in a very short time frame. Maybe this is the struggle that the Apostle Paul was describing when he admitted one minute to doing what is right, the next what is wrong.[32]

Eric Liddell will be remembered as 'the man who wouldn't run on Sunday', but his passion went beyond his sabbath beliefs. This is clearly portrayed in Hollywood's version of Liddell's greatest athletic achievement. Just before he runs for Olympic Gold in the 400m race, the so-called 'New York Thunder Bolt' gives Liddell a folded, handwritten note that reads, "'It says in the old Book. 'He that honours me I will honour.' Good Luck – Jackson Schultz." Not that Liddell needed luck; his belief was in the God who made him fast.

32. Romans 7:7–25.

In a symbolic act, the film director has Liddell clutching the piece of paper on the starting line and then again as he crosses the finishing line. However, the observant amongst us will have seen the apparent lack of film continuity; whenever the camera cuts to Liddell running the race, his hand is empty. Maybe that is prophetic! For while there may be times in our life when we lose touch with the purpose for which we do what we do, it is how we finish that truly matters. For all's well that ends well!

The film title, *Chariots of Fire*, is from a line in the hymn 'Jerusalem'. If you watch England playing cricket, you will sing, "Bring me my chariot of fire." The phrase is a biblical term. In 2 Kings, the prophet Elijah, at the end of his life, is taken up to heaven in a chariot of fire.[33] In short, he finished well, with the help of God's indwelling power.

In the film, Eric Liddell preaches a sermon based on Isaiah 40, reminding us how God enables us to "run and not grow weary".[34] With God's help, we can become a quiet revolutionary, a culture creator, and we can finish well.

Just prior to this moment, we are given a picture of Elisha and Elijah walking together. "Suddenly a chariot and horses of fire came between them and Elijah went up in a whirlwind to heaven."[35]

What a way to go!

---

33. 2 Kings 2:11.
34. Isaiah 40:31.
35. 2 Kings 2:11, MSG.

KEEPING IT REEL

Mistakes I Have Made:

- Being a reactor more than a responder.
- Running *from* more than running *for.*
- Failure to find my reason for being.
- Too much Abrahams, not enough Liddell.
- Being defined by what I do.

Lessons I Have Learnt:

- Passionate people do incredible things.
- Live with an awareness of calling.
- Consumed or consumer, we choose.
- To do whatever I do sensing God's pleasure.
- Live my immediate in the light of an ultimate.

CHAPTER

TRAILER

The Soloist (2009) is a powerful and emotive drama film about an African American violinist called Nathan Ayers (Jamie Foxx), living as a homeless man on the streets, and Steve Lopez (Robert Downey Jr.), a *Los Angeles Times* columnist and journalist who discovers Ayers and writes about him in his paper. Lopez, concerned about Ayers' mental health, tries to help him but his offers to improve the musician's life are not always either appropriate or appreciated. In many ways, *The Soloist* accordingly teaches us some important lessons about how to get alongside the lost, the last and the least. Any attempt to force them into becoming like us is patronising and unproductive. But truly getting alongside them, learning from them even when they only have two strings on which to play the instrument of their life, leads not only to them being changed, but us being changed too. *The Soloist*, based on the novel of the same name by Steve Lopez (and a true story), reminds us that we are called to be Alongsiders who listen and learn from those whom we're trying to help.

OUTSIDERS, INSIDERS
AND ALONGSIDERS

The Soloist

Whether because it's a true-life story, or because it portrays the unlikely relationship between a newspaper columnist and a homeless musician, few books have grabbed my attention like *The Soloist*.[36] Throughout my life, some books have been gamechangers. As a teenager searching for God knows what, Elizabeth Elliot's *Through Gates of Splendour* provided a *eureka* moment in an otherwise confused existence. More recently, Henri Nouwen's *The Return of the Prodigal* has challenged my legalist 'elder brother' attitude. Nouwen has not only opened my mind to the Father heart of God, but changed my watery, performance-orientated Christianity into the grace-filled new wine of biblical sonship.

That any book should have this transformative effect is amazing, considering my upbringing. When I was a child, my parents were more likely to introduce me to the world of cartoons and comics than the English classics. Having bookshelves full of Sunday school awards may have looked impressive, but the fact that they were all unread is evidence that, as a young boy, English literature was neither a pleasure nor a priority. Had it not been for an English teacher, who could hold a group of unruly teenagers spellbound, and had it not been for my studies at theological college, my love of the English language might still lie dormant.

The release of *The Soloist* happened to coincide with my involvement with an inner-city church in downtown Peoria,

36. Steve Lopez, *The Soloist*, Berkley Books, 2008.

Illinois, USA. This may have subconsciously created an appetite in me to read what Steve Lopez had to say about working with homeless people. Having pre-ordered my copy, I eagerly awaited a call from Barnes and Noble who, along with its in-house Starbucks, had created a regular and heady mix of literature and latté for me. I was now on first-name terms with the staff, who would often have my order ready before I reached the counter. With a large dry cappuccino and a cinnamon scone, I was in literary heaven.

To read a book in one sitting has only happened once in my life, but that is exactly what happened with *The Soloist*. Every one of its 289 pages had me engrossed. Buzz Bissinger nailed it when he wrote, "Many books claim to be about redemption and the affirmation of the human spirit, but they are false gospels. *The Soloist* is singularly and unforgettably true in all respects."[37]

It should therefore be no surprise that a film based on the book would make it into *The Reel Story*. Sadly, even though Jamie Foxx and Robert Downey Jr. are the principal actors in this film, few people have even heard of the book, let alone watched the film.

Life with a Two-string Violin

Built around the unlikely friendship between a *Los Angeles Times* columnist and a homeless street musician, the drama of *The Soloist* derives from this clash of different cultures. In their first meeting, Lopez leaves the comfort of his high-rise office and finds himself at ground level listening to a down-and-out trying to make music on a two-stringed violin. From this chance meeting an unusual relationship begins. While initially Lopez sees Nathaniel Ayers as material for a great column, over

---

37. Endorsement by Buzz Bissinger, author of *Friday Lights*, on the back cover of *The Soloist*.

time he finds himself stirred by a deep empathy for someone who has tragically lost their way in life.

The journey of these two men is fascinating and frightening in equal measure.

At times it seems that the columnist is trying to fast-track the musician into a more acceptable way of life as an 'insider' by coaxing him to take up residence in an apartment. Unable to embrace the street player's rough way of life, Lopez feels his redemption would be complete if he could only encourage him to come inside. It takes a while, but eventually the columnist comes to a place of understanding: the musician is not meant to come inside to where he is. Lopez is meant to go outside to where the musician is. That is where he is going to learn that life can be lived to the full even with just two strings. When life is reduced to making ends meet, living with just two strings is your reality. This can happen to anyone, including the columnist.

A Prophetic Picture

You're probably getting the idea by now: movies are metaphors for my life. And *The Soloist* is no exception. For me, it provides a picture of what is known as *evangelism*; spreading the Good News about Jesus Christ. Christians are people called to spread news, and in that respect the newspaper columnist in the movie is a great symbol of that. We too work for the news. The Good News!

The trouble is, like Steve Lopez, we are not very good at reaching out to those outside the Church.

It may be an over-simplification, but evangelism today has been reduced to an exercise of simply finding ways of getting *outsiders* to come *inside* – that is, to join and regularly attend a weekend religious gathering. For me, *The Soloist* is a picture of what we are doing wrong, as well as what we need to do if we want to do it right.

Let's look at the film's plot using the language of insiders, outsiders and (forgive the rather clumsy, made-up word) 'Alongsiders'. Broadly speaking, the story involves four principal acts, and in all of these it is the reporter Lopez's changing behaviour that is important. We will apply these to the Church's attempts to spread the Good News about Jesus.

Act 1   When the Insider fails to go outside.

Act 2   When the Insider insists on the Outsider coming inside.

Act 3   When the Outsider fails to come inside.

Act 4   When the Insider becomes the Alongsider.

The Four Scenarios

First Scenario: when the Insider fails to go outside. To see a lasting change in the complex, multi-layered lives of the Nathaniel Ayers of this world, Christ-followers are going to need to behave differently and indeed more radically. Changing lives is not a quick-fix solution. You can't just shout to the outsider to come inside. Insiders need to be in it for the long haul and go out to where the outsiders live and work. The first word of the Great Commission that Jesus gave to his disciples was "Go!" Jesus didn't tell them to stay put and wait for the outsiders to come to them. No, the Great Commission was a 'Go to Them', not a 'Come to Us' mandate. Insiders therefore need to stop believing that simply staying in church and organising regular seeker services is somehow going to produce a Great Awakening. It is not! Insiders will never see anything close to revival while they stay indoors. As Christians, we have got to learn to get out more and be among the lost, the least and the lonely.

Second Scenario: when the Insider insists on the Outsider coming in. Let me paint a picture for you.

He stands silhouetted against the afternoon sun, a well-dressed middle-aged man whose 1950s attire looks more suited to the role of an undertaker than a street preacher. Although his dress sense is somewhat understated, the same cannot be said of his rough, gravelly voice. Without the aid of a sound system, his words bellow out across the busy intersection of the small mining community. With the confidence of a drill sergeant and the clarity of a police siren, this well-known religious figure refuses to be put off by the noisy traffic or by people's indifference. Interspersing each volley of biblical texts with references to the spiritual state of mankind, he punctuates his sentences with words like, "God", "sin", "death", "hell" and "judgement". What his religious rant lacks in structure, he makes up for with volume. And for those unfortunates caught in the crossfire, their options are limited. Either pay him no attention or make a hasty retreat in the opposite direction. Making the street corner his pulpit and the pedestrians his congregation, he works on the premise that if the people won't come to church then the church must come to the people. As most of the foot traffic works in the local coalmine, this intrusion into their leisure time is creating a great deal of hostility. Sunday afternoon is a time to relax, not wrestle with the judgemental words of a lone street preacher.

But the preacher is not alone! Feeling like someone wearing a sandwich board that on one side reads, 'The End of the World is Nigh' and on the other, 'Prepare to meet Thy Doom', I have somehow been coerced into partnering with the preacher. The plan is to catch people in a pincer movement. While the preacher stands on one side of the road, I stand on the other distributing religious leaflets. The assumption is that people will be so challenged by the words of the sermon that they will gladly accept a free pamphlet. How wrong can a person be! More out of pity than persuasion, some people do take a tract. Any satisfaction this response might have given me is soon deflated when I later spot many of these pamphlets littering the streets.

This is what I mean by *the insider insisting that outsiders come in*; whether partnering with a street preacher, cold-selling Christianity at people's front doors, performing street art, or touring the neighbourhood with a huge sound system strapped to the roof of a car, I've been there, done that, and got the corny Christian t-shirt to prove it. No wonder evangelism became associated in my mind with red-faced embarrassment. Don't get me wrong, I wholeheartedly embrace the Great Commission where Jesus said, "Go then and make disciples of all nations,"[38] but the method of insisting that outsiders should come in is flawed and ineffective in today's world. While Christ's message is unchanging, the Church's methods have often failed to change. That is proving near fatal in terms of the growth of the Church.

It Takes Time

When the author Noel Coward was asked if he believed in God, he replied, "We've never been properly introduced."[39]

---

38. Matthew 28:19, AMP.
39. https://www.thegoodbook.co.uk/common/productfiles/cxph-Talk%20Transcript%20Week%202.pdf

This is the challenge. Introducing our friends to a loving heavenly father will take more than a one-off event hosted by a few excitable preachers. It takes quality time to build genuine friendships and relationships, forged in an atmosphere of approval, appreciation and acceptance. Jesus devoted three years of His life to walk and talk with twelve people He wanted to be with.[40] Using everyday life as a classroom, Jesus the Rabbi took time to turn a group of unknowns into a team of world-class players. Discipleship – or developing devoted followers of Jesus – is not achieved in an instant.

In *Outliers*, Malcolm Gladwell talks about 'The 10,000 Hour Rule'. He reckons that it takes roughly ten thousand hours of practice to reach a level of excellence. Quoting the neurologist Daniel Levitin, he writes, "ten thousand hours of practice is required to achieve the level of mastery associated with being a world-class expert – in anything."[41] It takes time to excel.

Whether it's becoming a musician, sportsperson, writer or a master criminal, to achieve true mastery requires a high level of commitment.

In order to become a fully qualified carpenter and joiner, a person in times past would have needed to serve a five-year apprenticeship. By working alongside and observing a master craftsman, an apprentice would grow in their understanding and expertise. Eventually, the pupil would be released to practice their craft and in time train others. Five days a week, eight hours a day, an apprentice would watch the master at work; a long-haul lesson that roughly equates to 'The 10,000-Hour Rule'.

---

40. Mark 3:13, 14, ESV.
41. Malcolm Gladwell, Outliers. *The Story of Success*, Little, Brown & Company, 2008, p.40.

Jesus chose twelve ordinary guys to be "apprenticed to Him".[42] Over a period of three-and-a-half years, or approximately ten thousand hours, He invested His time and energy in them, an investment that would ultimately pay dividends in the life of each disciple.

Time is a precious commodity, which is why the Apostle Paul encourages us to "make the most of time" and "buy up every opportunity". Or, as another Bible translation puts it, "Be wise in your behaviour towards non-Christians, and make the best possible use of your time. Speak pleasantly to them, but never sentimentally, and learn to give a proper answer to every questioner."[43]

Credit where credit is due; at least Steve Lopez was willing to leave the security of his LA office and get involved with those on the outside. This is where *The Soloist* becomes painful. I am one of those Christian ghetto dwellers, or desert islanders, who loves his own company and finds time alone a real pleasure. It is not that I hate people, but when it comes to socialising, I can soon become 'peopled out'. My wife Tina is totally different; too long on her own and she needs a people fix. Sadly, I've become infected with what social researchers call "cocooning".[44]

The earliest Christians were a bit like that. They were told by Jesus in Acts 1:8 to wait until the power of the Holy Spirit filled them and then they would go out as His witnesses in ever-increasing circles, from Jerusalem to Judea, from Judea to Samaria, and from Samaria to the ends of the earth. The only problem was that they liked the first part (about being supernaturally empowered) but they clearly didn't like the second part (about going out and being effective witnesses to Jesus). If we're honest, we're no different!

It should be no surprise to learn that in Acts 8:1 persecution came. Non-Christians started arresting and even killing

---

42. Matthew 5:1, MSG.
43. Colossians 4:5, 6, J. B. Phillips.
44. *The Popcorn Report*, Harper Collins, 1992, Faith Popcorn, p.27.

Christians. While God didn't cause this to happen, He did allow it. Why? The answer is in Acts 8:1. This persecution resulted in the first Christians being dispersed. Guess where! Throughout Samaria to the ends of the earth! *They were all scattered throughout the regions of Judea and Samaria.*[45] So, what's the lesson? It's this. If you employ a gathered approach to evangelism, you'll likely end up being scattered!

Those Stubborn Outsiders

Third Scenario: when Outsiders refuse to come inside. In his book *Breakout*, which won Christianity magazine's Book of the Year in 2010, Mark Stibbe describes how at the start of his time leading St Andrew's Church, Chorleywood, he employed a 'come to us' approach to evangelism. He ran an Alpha Course for those in his community who might be interested in Christianity, and regular Sunday evening seeker services with the leading evangelist in the UK, Canon J. John (then a member of Mark's church). The only problem was that non-Christians didn't come to either. The first Alpha Course had five non-Christians in it. The seeker services simply attracted large numbers of people who were already Christians and who believed that these servicers were going to be a lot livelier than the ones in their own churches. Something was wrong with the model. Outsiders were being obstinate; they were refusing to come inside.

Then, Andrew Williams, Mark's associate vicar and co-author of *Breakout*, came up with the idea of going out into the local area with mission-shaped communities. These met in school halls, scout huts, coffee shops and clubs. Some served neighbourhoods. Others served special groups, such

---

45. Acts 8:1.

as the homeless, the learning disabled, the creatives, the deaf, and so on. Pretty soon, non-Christians started joining these mission-shaped communities in large numbers, not because they were being invited to a gathered place, but because they were being served where they were, in their own place. At the end of Mark's time at St Andrew's, there were thirty-two of these mission-shaped communities with 1,700 members. His last Alpha Course was attended by 126 non-Christians, all of whom were invited by their friends who had gone out and served them. Every one of them decided to become a follower of Jesus.

You see the difference? While we stay indoors and shout the message, outsiders will mostly refuse to come inside. But once insiders start going to outsiders, all things are possible. As Mark Stibbe puts it, when we transition from cruise-ship church to lifeboat church, then we will see revival, just as he did.

We must therefore resist the spiritual version of "cocooning" – "the impulse to go *inside* when it just gets too tough and scary *outside*".

The only thing that holds us back here is fear. We are very afraid of going out and meeting people who don't talk our language and hold to our beliefs. It's a challenge, to say the least. We are fearful of rejection, disapproval, getting it wrong, messing up the message, letting God – a whole bunch of things! But the Bible tells us to choose faith, not fear. Once we choose faith over fear, then we too can experience our breakout, and see the lost, the last and the least coming to know Jesus.

Maybe we can see a similar dynamic in cinemas. Given that this book is about films, this is not such a bad idea. Today, cinema attendance is in decline. Those in charge of the cinema chains are consequently going to great lengths to modernise their image and maximise visitor attraction. Innovative upgrades include plush seating that pitches you into a near horizontal position, a glass of wine and nachos delivered to your seat, big screens, 2D, 3D, or 4D, massive speaker systems, and so on. Seats have been created in some cinemas which are able to move viewers, pump smells and spray water to reflect the action on the screen.

Will this work? Probably not. Today, people are changing their habits rapidly and dramatically. No longer are they travelling to gather in the cinema. They are staying indoors, investing in large TVs and elaborate sound systems, creating a home cinema. Subscribing to Netflix, Amazon Prime, Sky and other service providers, today's viewers would rather stay at home and eat nachos with their friends.

And who can blame them? They can watch endless TV series that have the production qualities of the best movies, and at a fraction of the price and with none of the inconvenience. If you don't believe me, do some research into the *Game of Thrones* phenomenon. Season 8, the final season of the show, contained six episodes that are almost film length, and whose special effects are better than what people are used to seeing at movie theatres. Today, then, movie-watchers are voting with their feet. They have transitioned from being gathered in one place to being dispersed in multitudes of homes

The Church needs to learn from this. Being gathered and putting on something entertaining is not going to work. If the church tries to compete with the expertise of the entertainment industry, it will justly be accused of being a copycat culture and it will fall far short every time. Those outside will continue to refuse to come inside if we do that. We just can't compete with HBO or MGM, with stand-up comedians and dynamic political orators, with Ariane Grande and Mumford & Sons.

We don't have the human resources and we don't have the material resources either.

No, the answer lies in what cinema can never give people – authentic relationships and alternative communities. These have been one of the great strengths of genuine Christianity since the time of Jesus. They are profoundly attractive when they are working as they were always intended to work, with people going out into their local villages, towns and cities and serving the lost, the last and the least with the *saving* Gospel (preaching the life-changing message about Jesus), the *social* Gospel (bringing justice to those who have no voice) and the *supernatural* Gospel (praying for the sick in Jesus' name and seeing miracles).

The Fourth Dimension

Fourth Scenario: when the Insider becomes the Alongsider. As I look back over some of the more questionable methods I've used to introduce people to the Christian faith, I find myself resonating with the lyrics of that Bono song, 'I Still Haven't Found What I'm Looking For'. At least, that was true for many years. But then I experienced a revelation that had me running naked through the streets of my mind like some modern-day Archimedes crying, "Eureka! Eureka! I have found it!"

This lightbulb moment came when reading a phrase first coined by the late Michael Green.

Speaking of how the first-century, persecuted Christians were scattered throughout the then known world, Green describes how they shared the Good News concerning the risen Christ. This is what he wrote: "This must often have been not formal preaching, but *the informal chattering to friends* and chance acquaintances, in home and wine shops, on walks, and around market stalls. They were everywhere *gossiping the Gospel;* they did it naturally, enthusiastically, and with the conviction of those who are not paid to say that sort of thing. Consequently, they were taken seriously, and the movement spread."[46]

Eureka! The word 'chattering', along with the phrase 'gossiping the Gospel', was enough to lead me to create an online resource called *Coffee Chats.*[47] What Green coined in these words was the green light (forgive the pun) for which I'd been waiting. Here was the Great Commission in its simplest form, permission for a mission that made sharing our faith normal, relaxed, real and authentic; a process that encouraged me to count *conversations* rather than *conversions.* The idea of informally chatting to friends gives us permission to be part of a ground force movement that, in reaching out to others, is supernaturally natural and naturally supernatural. Rather than dumping a whole truckload of theological truths on some unsuspecting individual, we try instead to notice people, to enter their world, walk with them, get to know them and befriend them as fellow human beings rather than projects that need fixing.

Within our spheres of influence, we all have people who are friendly enough to have a chat with us. So, what if we thought of three people with whom we could have coffee, without it feeling weird, three individuals we'd like to get to know better, with no hidden agenda. This is what we call *The Three Friends Challenge.* Jesus taught us to "Use [our] worldly resources to benefit others and to make friends."[48] Maybe the drinks should be on us!

---

46. Michael Green, *Evangelism in the Early Church*, William B. Eerdmans Publishing Company, 2003, p.243. Emphasis original.
47. www.coffeechats.org
48. Luke 16:9b, NLT.

In this sort of approach, evangelism is completely transformed from being something fearful into something accessible to all. Instead of it being a crisis event (getting someone to say the sinner's prayer), it becomes a process, a matter of loving people over a long period of time. Instead of it being done by professionals (paid evangelists), this is something that can be done by amateurs, which is a French word meaning 'lovers'. Anyone who loves God and loves people can do this. The key is to accept the call to be an *Alongsider*. This call is for all who are prepared to come alongside those outside the Church, whether they are far away from God, or at the very cusp of a life-changing decision to follow Jesus. If you're an insider, it's time to become an Alongsider! This is what Steve Lopez had to learn to embrace in *The Soloist*.

The Great Alongsider

As a newly married couple, we did not have enough funds to purchase a reliable vehicle. Cold winter mornings were therefore often a challenge for the car we had. Having scraped the frost from the windows and prised open the frozen driver's door, I could finally insert the ignition key and fire up our tired-looking 1960s Ford Anglia Saloon. Sadly, this often failed, and a quick diagnosis would tell my non-mechanical brain that the battery was dead. With no time for a post-mortem, I needed to call a friend, one with a fully functioning car. This trusty, bleary-eyed mate would draw his vehicle alongside mine. Once we'd made the connection between his battery and mine, my failed power source would draw energy from his to kickstart my engine back into life. This single act of friendship was enough to enable me to continue my journey.

This simple story illustrates perfectly the life of a person we're calling an Alongsider. He or she is someone whose trustworthy friendship enables them to come alongside others to make a relational connection that in time may kickstart a conversation about spiritual matters. As such, Alongsiders portray godly characteristics that will verbally and non-verbally strengthen and support those who have either stalled or failed to start their quest for spiritual truth.

If you think about it, Jesus was the ultimate Alongsider. Walking between twenty and twenty-five miles a day, Jesus travelled the equivalent of almost the entire circumference of the earth. Except for the very occasional use of a donkey, He went most of the time on foot. Rather than seeing the Galilean countryside as an inconvenience, He used it as a teaching opportunity. Those apprenticed to Him would follow closely, listening and learning from everything their teacher said and did. This 'following closely' was done by the students of other Rabbis too and gave rise to a Jewish blessing: "May you be covered in the dust of your Rabbi."[49]

Jesus didn't just draw alongside His followers. He also came alongside the outsiders, the disenfranchised. Stepping into places religious leaders refused to enter, Jesus shared meals with people with whom others refused to associate. He drew alongside lepers, beggars, prostitutes and tax collectors. He connected with the lost, the last and the least in order to kickstart a conversation that enabled them to continue their journey towards God.

When Christ-followers become cocooned in their church environment, making friends with those who think and behave differently can be challenging.

---

49. Tim Bartee, "May you be covered with the dust of your Rabbi." Sidney Daily News, 2016.

In order to break out of their 'Christian-only Zone', some use everyday activities to initiate a conversation. Dog walkers find it easy to talk with other dog lovers. Parents find their children are the catalyst for striking up a conversation with other parents. Lovers of music use theatres in the same way foodies use restaurants to chat with people of similar interests.

Sometimes it requires a little more effort to break out of our cloistered environments. We can use personal interests like gardening, fishing, writing, sewing, soft furnishings, vintage cars and exercise. We've used pubs and clubs to mix with people we'd otherwise never have the opportunity of meeting. When we co-work with the Great Alongsider, the opportunities to make friends are endless. It simply requires our availability.

The good news is that we do not do this alone, nor in our own strength. As the greatest Alongsider of all time prepared to leave, He promised His graduates that He would send another Alongsider just like Him.[50] The Holy Spirit is described as "one called alongside to help", so this companionship lifestyle was set to continue.

Seizing the Moment

As your eyes meet across a crowded room, the stranger seems to give an unsolicited smile. As they make their way towards you, your mind begins to rehearse the opening lines of what promises to be a fascinating conversation. Thinking you're the sole focus of their interest, you're shocked when your "hello" isn't reciprocated in the way you expected. It soon becomes clear that the person they really wanted to speak to is standing behind you. But that individual is otherwise engaged, so you become a convenient stop-off point, a pause in their pursuit of someone more interesting, more important, more influential than you.

---

50. See John 14:16.

Whether a casual acquaintance or long lost friend, Alongsiders acknowledge, appreciate and accept everyone on equal terms.

If we're encouraged to "make the most of every opportunity . . . to bring out the best in others in a conversation",[51] then surely the first step is to *notice* people.

In his excellent book, *The Nine Arts of Spiritual Conversation*, John Crilly writes, "Do we want to live like Jesus, to notice people and have compassion toward them? Noticing people can move us to compassion and action as it humanises the nameless faces around us. People become real to us, with real lives and real problems in need of a real Savior."[52]

In the busyness of everyday life, it's so easy to miss the moment: a breath-taking sunset, a baby's smile, a child's first game, a teenager's question, a partner's loving look, a friend's cry for help, an amazing vista. When it comes to social interactions, it's possible to be physically present, yet mentally absent.

Jesus was present in every moment, whether it was with the wealthy or the poor, with the businessman or the beggar. It didn't matter if He was attending a party or a wake, whether He was asleep in a boat or standing on the seashore, He was always present. When Zacchaeus climbed a tree, when blind Bartimaeus cried out, when Peter sank in the storm, when Thomas verbalised his doubts and when a mother grieved the loss of a son, Jesus noticed and was there. Jesus truly was the ultimate Alongsider. He seized every moment by being fully present in every moment, whoever He was with at the time.

So, let's go chat.

---

51. Colossians 4:5, 9, MSB.
52. Mary Schaller and John Crilly, *The 9 Arts of Spiritual Conversations*, Tyndale House Publishers, 2016, p.45.

"For Christians living in this technologically interconnected but relationally disconnected culture, engaging in simple conversational practices will communicate the unconditional love of Christ to people all around us and could reverse the downward spiral of our churches."[53]

It's Time to Go

We started with music (*The Soloist*) so we'll end with it too. Ben Zander is the conductor of the Boston Philharmonic Orchestra and, along with his wife Rosamund, he teaches a class on leadership called *The Art of Possibility*.[54] As part of this excellent programme, Ben tells of the story of a fellow conductor, Herbert von Karajan. As the principal conductor of the Berlin Philharmonic, life for Herbert is extremely busy. So much so that one day, having finished his rehearsal, he rushed outside, jumped into his limousine and shouted at his driver, "Hurry, hurry, go, go, drive, drive, go, go!" "Very good sir," the driver said, "but where to?" To which Herbert von Karajan replied, "Doesn't matter, they need me everywhere!"

When all is said and done, we need to *go*. We need to go everywhere because those living within our sphere of influence need us. They need us to come alongside them and build genuine friendship.

In conclusion:

- Identify the Soloists in your existing sphere, the people you're called to come alongside.

- Pray that God will help you build relational bridges with them.

- Show genuine interest in your Soloists, remembering that they are *people* not *projects*.

53. Ibid., p.25.
54. Ben and Roz Zander, *An Art of Possibility No. 1 & No. 2* DVD, Groh Productions, Chicago, Illinois.

- Look for opportunities to casually chat with them. Then chat, chat and chat some more about whatever interests them.

- Demonstrate acts of kindness to your Soloists and when God prompts and/or they ask, 'gossip the Gospel' in a relaxed, non-religious, non-threatening way. Use your own words and your own faith story. Remember that our stories are powerful tools that we often underestimate!

- Use resources to help you, for example, www.coffeechats.org.

KEEPING IT REEL

Mistakes I Have Made:
- Missing God-given opportunities.
- Treating people as projects to fix.
- Distancing myself from those who believe and behave differently.
- Seeing success as people on seats, not lives transformed.
- Making misguided judgements on external behaviour.

Lessons I have Learnt:
- Be present in the moment.
- To be *insulated* not *isolated* from the world.
- To walk in another person's shoes before judging them.
- Count conversations not conversions.
- It's possible to be technologically connected yet relationally disconnected.

CHAPTER

TRAILER

Toy Story (1995) is a computer-animated feature film about a group of toys that pretend to be lifeless when their human owner, Andy, is around, but come to life when he's out of the room. Led by Woody (Tom Hanks), these toys engage in an extraordinary act of collaborative ingenuity to be reunited with Andy when he and his family move house. In many ways, this is a parable about the company that produced this pioneering film – Pixar. The hundred or so people who worked on *Toy Story* did so at a time when films were moving on from old, set ways to new ones. These people worked together and produced a compelling new vision for animated films. This, in turn, is a prophetic picture of what the Church needs today. The creatives need to be given permission to use their anointed gifts of innovation to take us out of an old, set way of doing things into a new era of innovation. We need to catch up with Jesus, the true creative. He's moving house and He believes in going "to infinity and beyond!" Truly, it's time for a Pixar generation in the Church. We're not alone in this. Jesus' song over us is, 'You've Got A Friend In Me'!

CREATIVE GENIUS

Toy story

It shouldn't surprise anyone that a film about animated toys has made the final cut of this book. *Toy Story* showcases a quality that is almost universally admired. I'm talking about *creative genius*. There is no doubt that when Pixar produced *Toy Story*, they broke the mould. With follow-on movies like *A Bug's Life* (1998), *Toy Story 2* (1999), *Monsters, Inc.* (2001), *Finding Nemo* (2003), *The Incredibles* (2004), *Cars* (2006), *Ratatouille* (2007), and *WALL-E* (2008), Pixar's creative genius is truly remarkable and unparalleled. Pixar has achieved all this in a collective way, working against the grain in the modern entertainment industry, realising that the environment you create determines the product you produce. In the process, Pixar opened the curtain on the future and stepped into it.

For me, this is something to lament as well as celebrate. On the one hand, I want to give a big shout out to Pixar's extraordinary technological innovation. On the other hand, when I think of the Church, it's hard not to be disappointed. In comparison with companies like Pixar, the Church has lagged way behind. Pixar had an almost prophetic sense of what kinds of stories were needed in the future, and what sort of animation could serve these stories. The Church, in stark contrast, is constantly playing catch-up. Worse still, Christians seem to veer from being suspicious of creativity to being neglectful of it. Far from being pioneers and trailblazers in the areas of artistic creativity and technological innovation, as we were at one time in Western history, we are now way behind.

There is no doubt in my mind that the Church has moved away from the leading to the trailing edge of spiritual and social enterprise and it has done so by marginalising creativity. At one time in the past, Christianity was instrumental in birthing education, healthcare and social enterprise, becoming one of the major players in the Industrial Revolution. Where are the prophetic entrepreneurs today? And if they do exist, will the Church give them credence? Will it honour what they're doing?

Christianity needs men and women who will peer through the curtain into the future and help us travel there.

Christianity needs a Pixar generation if we're to see a move of God that truly changes the culture around us.

Copycat Crimes

While Martin Luther King Jr. had a dream, I have this recurring nightmare in which Western churches are committing 'copycat crimes' every weekend. The scene of the crime is often a darkened stage, with blackout curtains, flashing lights and smoke machines – a familiar sight in many megachurches. Incorporating keyboard, guitar, drums and singers, large and small churches mimic these megachurches in almost every facet of worship. With a worship-set more committed to performance than participation, congregations every Sunday observe the same crime being committed on stage.

What is that crime? It is the crime of copycatting what is going on in the entertainment industry outside in the world. Failing to have the originality to create something new, the megachurches simply mimic what the world is doing, and smaller churches then follow their lead, copycatting the copycats. Even in the dress code and stage-setting, these megachurches simply replicate what the world is doing far better and, in the process, become the chief suspects in what in creative terms is criminal. With lyrics that all sound the same, the songs lack both the depth and originality of what the world outside the Church is producing. Everything within the Church's version smacks of stale imitation. Where is what my old university professor used to call, 'the uniqueness of otherness'?

When I look back to Old Testament times, it's hard not to be sad at how far we've declined when it comes to creative genius. In the time of Moses, the people of God were wandering in the desert when the Holy Spirit filled an artist called Bezalel. The Book of Exodus tells us that this anointing was for the specific task of creating the Tabernacle in which God's presence was going to reside. This Tabernacle was to be aesthetically beautiful, befitting its purpose, which was to host the most precious thing in the world – the manifest glory of God. Bezalel was endowed with the ability to design and build something beautiful.

It's striking that the first person in the Bible to be specifically described as being 'filled with the Holy Spirit' is an artist, and that the purpose of this infilling was to do with creative genius. Bezalel, with the help of Oholiab, constructed a Tabernacle according to heaven's blueprint, and what they and the entire people of God created became the gathering place which welcomed the glory of God's manifest presence.[55] All this then encourages us to ask the question: where are the people like Bezalel in today's Church? Where are the men and women filled with the Holy Spirit for the purpose of creativity?

---

55. Exodus 31.

Where are the leaders like Moses who encourage the creatives to build a landing zone for the glory of God?

Where are the new songs? Where are the heavenly scribes, the anointed writers, who are being released in the Church to bring out things old and new?[56]

The problem with the criminal act of copycatting the world is this: it creates the sense that everything we do is the exact opposite of *Toy Story*. It lacks innovation. It lacks what one BBC TV series, devoted to modern art, called *The Shock of the New*. Everything feels same-old. Everything feels staid. Instead of the fresh bread of God's presence, warm and fragrant, we have old bread whipped out of the freezer, cold and bland. What we need today are prophetic figures, people who can redirect rather than reflect contemporary culture. We need God's Renaissance generation. We need people like John the Baptist, an original Renaissance Man. He stood on the hinge of history and bridged the gap between the old and the new. Commenting on this man's ministry and methods, Jesus announced to the crowd, "He was not what you expected was he?"[57] When, in a positive sense, was the last time people leaving our Sunday gatherings excitedly said, "I didn't expect that!"? Just as when the Queen of Sheba visited the kingdom of Solomon, visitors to our Sunday gatherings should experience a 'Wow Factor' as they step into the beautiful and glorious presence of God.

God is infinitely creative, and we are by nature creative just like Him.

56. Matthew 13:52.
57. See Matthew 11:7–19.

When we come to Christ and are filled with the Spirit of adoption (Romans 8:15), we declare that God is our Abba, our Heavenly Dad, and in the process, we become His sons and daughters. As this happens, we discover that our real identity is not based on our performance, but on our honoured position as God's royal children. This then releases us from what the Bible calls 'slavery', that striving to earn value through performance, and it sets us free to enjoy the Father's approval for who we are, not what we do. In this place of rest, we find not only our real identity but also our true creativity. Out of our bellies, the Holy Spirit begins to flow like a river, and in that river, there are songs, symphonies, stories, sculptures, and so on. The lesson then is obvious: Christians need to stop going to the world for its creative inspiration and start relying and drawing upon the Word of God and the Holy Spirit, the wellspring of true innovation.

All this means that we need to empty ourselves of the desire to perform and imitate and instead become empty vessels – people filled with, well, nothing. When chaos and darkness covered the earth, God revealed himself as Creator. It was out of nothingness that the creativity of heaven was demonstrated on earth. We need to become nothing. We need to let go of all our self-sufficiency and our dependency on the world's way of being creative, and we need to let God's creative genius, which resides within us all, have its way.

Raiders of the Lost Art

Why is it that Christianity lost its way when it comes to creative genius? Why is it, when you remember that it led the way during the Renaissance, that the Church lags far behind in scientific and artistic innovation? Maybe it's because of the Reformation; this movement not only realigned theology, it also suppressed the creativity of the Renaissance.

In 2018, Europe commemorated the 500th anniversary of the Reformation, when one man, Martin Luther, nailed a discussion paper to a church door that sparked a religious revolution still reverberating today. But before the Reformation, there was a movement known as the Renaissance. Indeed, the scientific and artistic innovations of the fifteenth century were essential for the theological advances in the sixteenth century and beyond. Without the invention of the printing press in Germany in the fifteenth century, Martin Luther would never have been able to have the impact he did as a writer one hundred years later.

In the Church today, we bandy about words like Revival, Restoration, Refreshing, Renewal and Reformation, but what about Renaissance? Do we not see that the Reformation had to be preceded and accompanied by a Renaissance? And do we not see what the Holy Spirit is doing today, releasing and raising up a new generation of creative people within the Church? Do we not see the fresh wind of the Spirit blowing across those sons and daughters who carry a passion for the creative arts? Do we not see the rebirth (the meaning of the word "Renaissance") of dance, music, song, storytelling, and art?

The truth is that the Reformation was a mixed blessing when it came to creativity. Take music. Martin Luther brought music from being appreciated only for its artistic merit to bearing the heft of sacred text, telling the biblical story, and conveying heavenly truth. A great lover of music, Luther ushered in a universal priesthood in which all believers could sing God's songs. When it came to art and sculpture, however, these were suppressed out of a fear that they would become objects of worship rather than aids to worship. A campaign of destroying religious imagery soon swept throughout Europe.

Thankfully, the picture is changing today. One of the Christians who has pioneered this transformation is Henri Nouwen. Studying a painting by Rembrandt depicting the

Return of the Prodigal Son, Nouwen had a life-changing revelation of the Father heart of God, and he passed this onto the Church in one of the most beautiful books ever written – *The Return of the Prodigal Son,* named after the painting. Like Bezalel, Nouwen created something artistic and aesthetic that became the vehicle for the presence of God. Through his God-given creativity, and reliant on Rembrandt's God-given creativity, Nouwen became a Renaissance Man, releasing in the process a new generation of Renaissance men and women who have breathed in the same fresh and clean air of the Holy Spirit. See how potent the arts can be when they are harnessed to the wind of the Holy Spirit?

Maligned, abused and misunderstood, the creatives within the Church have for too long in the past struggled to be heard.

But things are changing. What the Reformation despised or neglected, the Church today needs to recognise and redeem. However, this does not mean producing pale imitations of what the world is doing. Christian creatives are not called to be thermometers but thermostats. We are not to react like thermometers, simply reflecting the temperature of what worldly creatives are doing. We are to play the part of a thermostat and change the temperature of the entire culture. By nature, I am more of a thermometer than a thermostat. Commenting on what's already going on is easy. Creating heavenly alternatives that change the culture, that's far more challenging. How about you? Do you critique what the world's doing? Or do you recreate what the Father is doing?

The Pixar Principle

This is where I believe *Toy Story* is so important. The world's first computer-animated feature movie, *Toy Story* became the forerunner of a whole series of animated blockbuster movies released from the Pixar stable. Critics heralded it as "inventive" (*The Times*), "brilliant" and "exultantly witty" (*The New York Times*) and "visionary" (*Chicago Sun-Times*). *The Washington Post* found this to be a movie worthy of comparison to *The Wizard of Oz*.[58]

Excellence rarely comes easy, and *Toy Story* is proof of that. The hundred or so men and women who worked tirelessly for five years refused to compromise their vision or diminish their passion. Fighting old school thinkers from Disney, who held to tried and tested beliefs that making a musical would guarantee box office success, they continued to break creative barriers and took Pixar to a place that at the time seemed impossible.

Releasing the creative genius within an organisation requires embracing something of the Pixar philosophy. If culture is 'the way we do things around here', then honesty, or what they preferred to call 'candour', is a core value to releasing what Pixar called 'collective creativity'. What a contrast to the Church! I have spent so many hours in team meetings observing those with extraordinary creativity sitting in silence. Afraid of being exiled from the team if they voice an alternative idea to the leader's, they chose to be quiet and, in the process, creativity became the victim. Not so in Pixar. They gave freedom to their people to comment and criticise. They embodied a healthy creative culture, and "a hallmark of a healthy creative culture is that its people feel free to share ideas, opinions, and criticisms. The lack of candour, if unchecked, ultimately leads to dysfunctional environments."[59]

---

58. Ed Catmull, *Creativity Inc.*, Transworld Publishers, 2014, pp.x–xi.
59. Ibid., p.86.

Silencing and side-lining the creatives in the Church has fostered a bland and boring institution that simply reflects and copies the culture rather than redeems and changes it. 'Blessed are those who go around in circles for they shall be called wheels' is an apt description of so much Christian activity.

Without revising the received truths of our faith, we need to find new ways to share the Christian message.

People looking in on the Church today see it as something archaic and irrelevant. Anything that is repetitive runs the risk of become mundane. Our way of sharing the message has lost its freshness. It's become a shadow of its former self and a stale, pale imitation of the world's methods.

Right now, I'm thinking of John (not his real name), a godly creative man who took pieces of scrap material and created magnificent pieces of art. Each unique piece carried a biblical message that not only engaged the onlooker but opened a door to conversations about spiritual matters with otherwise non-interested, non-church individuals. Misunderstood and marginalised by Christians and church leaders, John struggled to find a place of acceptance for his unique approach to communicating biblical truth. For years he was refused permission to exhibit in church halls. This drove him to the periphery of church circles. Today, John would not darken the doors of any Christian gathering. To those ministers responsible for marginalising John and the many like him, I have three words: Shame on you!

What this all serves to highlight is that Renaissance comes with a price tag and the cost for those who are forerunners can, as with John and his namesake John the Baptist, be high. Pixar as a company paid a price too. We focus on the end-product – movies like *Toy Story* – because that's all we see and know. Few, however, realise that Pixar's early years were marked by the constant threat of bankruptcy, losing millions of dollars year on year, even after the amazing success of *Toy Story*.

Pixar is in many ways a credit to the idea that says *the environment you create determines the people/product you produce.* The people involved in developing the Pixar model had themselves been green housed in an environment in which they were given the finance and freedom to think outside the box. When good people are given free rein, innovation runs wild and things become both risky and scary. But as one of my heroes once said, "The greatest danger in life, is not taking the adventure." That was uttered by George Mallory, possibly the first man to make it to the summit of Everest. Innovative thinking is both risky and scary, but Pixar seemed to embrace the danger in order to get to the summit.

Leading Outside the Lines

There is said to be a sign in Alaska that simply reads, "Choose your rut carefully; you'll be in it for the next two hundred miles." Refusing to compromise their creative ideas and follow the well-worn tracks of old school thinking, Pixar led outside the lines. This is a lesson for the Church. If creative people are to be recognised and released, it will require a shift in leadership styles. Raising the expectation levels among the creatives is not enough; leaders need to embrace and engage the creative gift. Without a change in thinking, history will repeat itself and the creative arts will look to the secular rather than the spiritual for inspiration.

Just as George Lucas and Steven Spielberg struggled to persuade the studios to embrace their untested ideas, and

Pixar had to stand its ground to get Disney to embrace the first feature film entirely animated on a computer, so old school leadership styles could leave Christian creatives out in the cold. When you read the story behind *Star Wars* – the determination of George Lucas to make a different kind of sci-fi movie aimed at 14- and 15-year-olds – some would say that it was as if he had seen into the future and had decided to go there. In an interview, Lucas said, "The reason I'm making *Star Wars* is that I want to give young people some sort of faraway exotic environment for their imaginations to run around in."[60] That is the work of the creative genius, to see beyond the present and give us the wherefore to step into the future. Prophetic creatives see and speak the future into being, bringing that future into the here-and-now. The problem is this: without apostolic leaders to recognise and release the prophetic creatives, the former run the risk of boring the church, while the latter have the potential to blow it to bits. The church needs the synergy between them to work so that it can showcase heaven's creative genius within a framework of true biblical community.

Christianity therefore needs leaders who will 'lead outside the lines' – men and women who will recognise the creative genius in those who illuminate and illustrate aspects of God's truth we are otherwise unable to see.

"Impossible," I hear you say.

Well, not really because, "In each generation God always has had those men [and women] whose framework of vision reached beyond the general consciousness to see God's larger purpose . . . Such men [and women] moved beyond the narrow vision of their own day."[61]

---

60. www.biography.com/news/george-lucas-star-wars-facts, p.2.
61. DeVern Fromke, *Unto Full Stature*, Foundation Publishers, 1985, p.39.

From Dancers to Da Vinci

I love to observe those who display the creative genius. My journey perhaps began with me watching my own father taking scrap pieces of exotic timber from World War II packing cases and creating pieces of furniture that have become family heirlooms. When we observe an artist taking base materials to produce a visual masterpiece, or a sculptor moulding clay into a thing of beauty, or an author creating worlds out of words, a composer making unforgettable melodies out of notes, we venture into the outer edges of God's creative genius.

I have tried to embrace creativity in my preaching and teaching. I have employed professional dancers to introduce a talk entitled, 'All God's Children Got Shoes'. I have spoken on 'Learning to Lean' from Proverbs 3,[62] along with an apt motorbike story, exiting the auditorium on the back of a Harley Davison. I have used a 32-foot by 10-foot picture of Leonardo da Vinci's *The Last Supper* for people to attach post-it-note prayers to it. I have asked a concert pianist to perform on a hired Steinway at a Bible College graduation and used a living statue to launch a book on fatherhood. I believe that a visual generation needs the creative genius to illustrate and illuminate biblical truth.

---

62. Proverbs 3:5–6.

My reason for venturing into the world of publishing was to use the medium of words to illustrate spiritual truth. My first book, *Eight Characteristics of Highly Effective Christians*, was written to illuminate the basic principles of entering and enjoying kingdom life through what is known as 'the Beatitudes'. Writing, printing and binding just seven hardback copies of *Trust God and Keep Your Powder Dry* was a Christmas gift to each of our children, telling the story of God's grace over a hundred years of Spicer family history. To celebrate the 100th anniversary of Father's Day, I wrote *No Perfect Fathers Here*.

More recently, my first venture into the realm of children's books, *JJ and the Big Bend*, was an attempt to help young people struggling with low self-esteem to discover the Father heart of God. All this has been to fulfil what Sandra Bowden wrote, "The artist's mission is to help all of us to see, in nature and human life, what the physical eye, unaided might never discern. Art is not merely illustration, but illumination."[63]

To me, God's truth needs a multifaceted approach if it is to engage people. I'm not alone. I look at and cheer on people like the dance troop using their skills to speak about human trafficking, the Olympic horse rider using her experience and expertise to rehabilitate abused horses, linking them with soldiers suffering PTSD, and the skateboarder seeking to connect with an unreached mission field by setting up a ministry called 'Holy-Rollers'.

Each of these people are using their God-given imagination to showcase God's creative genius.

Pure Imagination

Pixar, the originators of *Toy Story,* is a business built on imagination. Here a team of creative people were not only

---

63. Sandra Bowden, *The Vocation of the Artist*, www.ArtWay.eu.

given permission to dream, but also the time, space and resources to think outside the box without fear of rejection.

A vivid imagination was something of a prerequisite for working on the world's first feature film to be animated entirely by a computer. If Christianity is to engage with a visual generation, there must be a re-emergence of creative thinkers working alongside leaders who lead outside the well-worn tracks of the previous generation.

While God gave Moses a *plan*, he also gave him *creative people* to make the vision visible.

Some might shudder at the thought of encouraging Christians to embrace that aspect of the divine DNA that thinks in images, to engage in a process whereby we allow the heart and mind to work in concert to create pictures. However, we are not talking about the impure and the natural here, but the pure and the supernatural. A godly imagination that flows from a pure heart and a renewed mind can be both Holy Spirit *inspired* and biblically *informed*. Artists, poets, musicians, singers, dancers and preachers alike need to adopt this two-winged approach to the creative process; without it we will crash and burn, but with it we will soar to new levels of visual expression. Just as a songwriter submits their lyrics to a theologian to check for biblical correctness, creatives need to embrace the tension between being biblically informed and spiritually inspired. It's this collaborative approach to the creative process that will release the creative genius amongst us.

It's my belief that the best ideas are yet to come. We are on the cusp of a spiritual renaissance in which there will be elements of going *Back to the Future*. Pushing back on the performance mode of evangelical entertainment, Christianity will once again embrace the simple yet sublime reality of New Testament community. Congregational size will matter less than authentic relationships. Diversity will be celebrated. People more than programmes or projects will be embraced. An environment will be established in which composers, artists, poets, preachers, musicians, singers and choreographers will be given time to dream. This will be a community in which creatives are given permission to exercise a godly imagination that ultimately takes us to places we never thought possible.

In this creative process, God's *super* is added to our *natural*. A divine collaboration takes place in which the Holy Spirit interacts with our spirit to give us mind-blowing, heart-racing, eye-popping, ear-tingling ideas that glorify God and extend his kingdom. As Ed Catmull puts it, "What we can do is construct an environment that nurtures trusting and respectful relationships and unleashes everyone's creativity. If we get that right, the result is a vibrant community where talented people are loyal to one another and their collective work, everyone feels that they are part of something extraordinary."[64] To which we add, "Let's set the stage and bring on the creatives."

The Return of the Creatives

Another example of the creative genius is what I call 'The Soft Soap Story'. A God-fearing French chemist one night had a dream in which he saw a detailed chemical formula. Having no idea what it might create, he took his vision to the laboratory. Using only natural ingredients rather than recognised preservatives, the man created what would eventually be marketed as a unique hand cleanser – a product that had the ability to remove heavy industrial contaminates

---

64. Ed Catmull, "How Pixar Fosters Collective Creativity", *Harvard Business Review*, September 2008.

without removing, but rather enriching, the skins natural oils. Recommended by doctors, nurses and health workers, what the Frenchman created would not only clean the hands of engineering oil and printer ink, it would help soothe skin disorders like Eczema, Psoriasis, as well as clear and prevent Dermatitis in all working environments. For many global organisations with a large workforce, this became the hand cleanser of choice. The ramifications of the chemist's dream would have far reaching economic and social effects on those involved in its production, distribution and eventually those engineers and printers using it.

We should expect more of this in our own times. The renaissance of creativity in the Church is being accompanied by a renewal of prophecy – by a restoration of the gift of Pentecost, namely dreams and visions. We should remember that C.S. Lewis had dreams of lions before he wrote the *Narnia Chronicles*. He was, in many ways, a prototype for what God wants to do in the Church today and in the future. Who knows what we will dream about when the Church makes space for God-given creativity?

But what do we really mean by creativity? In its simplest form, it is "the quality of being creative" or "the ability to create".[65] It is often associated with being an out-of-the-box thinker. *Spiritual* creativity is more than this; it is a divine interaction between the Holy Spirit and our spirit causing us to create works of art that carry the presence of God in covert or overt ways – as when Bezalel created the furnishings for the Tabernacle, or when Jesus told stories known as parables, or when Rembrandt painted a stunning picture of the Father welcoming his prodigal son home, or when Henri Nouwen wrote a classic book about the Father heart of God, based on Rembrandt's painting. To present old biblical truths and

---

65. *Webster's Dictionary.*

heavenly patterns in fresh and unfamiliar ways is at the very heart of *spiritual* creativity.

Phil Cooke, a well-established filmmaker and media consultant, who happens to be a Christian, blogged recently, "In many ways I think artists and creatives have been misunderstood at best and largely ignored and even ostracised by the church, particularly the evangelical segment."[66] It's time for the prodigal creatives to come home from the far country. It's time for the Spirit-filled people like Bezalel to be welcomed from the circumference into the centre of the Church. The story of the Bible begins with an act of creation and ends with an act of recreation. God is super-creative and wants a Church that reflects this. Bezalel was one of a great number of people who were creative. Among the people of Israel who wandered in the desert, there were hundreds of thousands who were enlisted by Moses, along with Bezalel, to create a dwelling place for His glory, a dwelling place of artistic beauty. That time has come again.

There are many people in the Church who are naturally extremely gifted. What they need is the infilling of God's Spirit. They need God's *super* to be added to their *natural*. For that to happen, the Church needs to stop marginalising its creatives and engage instead in the Pixar philosophy of recognising, gathering and harnessing these out-of-the-box thinkers. As these people reach up to heaven and receive the blueprints and ideas that are there waiting for them, fresh expressions of the glory of God will be released on the earth, resulting in not only a new Renaissance but also a second Reformation.

God is about to show up in a new way and we need to embrace the inherent skills of the creatives because the creative arts are the best way of helping people to embrace hidden truths. My belief in this has never been stronger.

---

66. www.philcooke.com

It's time for a new generation of creatives to arise – one with the natural skills of the Pixar specialists, and the supernatural anointing of our Creator God!

KEEPING IT REEL

Mistakes I Have Made:
- Undervaluing the inherent, creative nature of God within us.
- Seeing creativity as a solo act rather that a collective enterprise.
- Allowing excellence to become a burden rather than a blessing.
- Refusing to celebrate difference and diversity.

Lessons I Have Learnt:
- What is refreshingly new today can become religiously old tomorrow.
- Creativity is born out of deficiency.
- Insecurity ruins creativity.
- Creativity is a collective act.
- The environment we create determines the people/product we produce.
- Perseverance pays dividends.

CHAPTER

TRAILER

The Devil Wears Prada is a 2006 US comedy drama based on the bestselling novel with the same title by Lauren Weisberger. Starring Meryl Streep as Miranda, the boss at a high-end fashion magazine, and Anne Hathaway as Andy, her new assistant, the film explores the journey Andy takes from the compliant underling of an abusive, performance-driven employer to the self-assured and independent woman who no longer craves her boss's approval. Compelled to take on an identity that is not her own, and to embrace a destiny that isn't hers either, Andy rebels when she realises that she is losing her soul in a Faustian pact with the Devil, all for the sake of money and power. Throughout the film, clothes function as a powerful metaphor for the way in which people conceal their true identity or subsume others' identities (many designers ironically allowed their clothes to be used in the movie, making it one of the most expensively costumed films in history). *The Devil Wears Prada* is not just a satirical exposé of the fashion industry, it is also a poignant exploration of the way we can so easily be seduced into a life of approval addiction in abusive social systems.

APPROVAL ADDICTION

The Devil Wears Prada

The Devil Wears Prada is a comedy-drama about a college graduate called Andy Sachs (Anne Hathaway) and her relationship with her boss Miranda Priestly (Meryl Streep). Having moved to New York, Andy takes on a job that she's told a million girls would die for. As co-assistant to the chief editor of Runway fashion magazine, Andy enters the new and challenging world of high-end fashion. Intensely demanding and notoriously difficult to work with, her boss succeeds in turning her dream job into a living nightmare. This is the dramatic core of the film. If drama is conflict, then there's plenty of it. The interactions between these two characters not only create the humour and drama of the film, they also set the backdrop for discussing a problem from which many people suffer – approval addiction.

As Andy begins to gain her boss's approval, she climbs the corporate ladder to become the number one assistant. However, in her quest to be honest and true to who she really is, Andy eventually quits her prestigious position to pursue her dream of becoming a journalist. Alongside the turbulent storyline and the well-developed humour, this is a film about being authentic – discovering your identity and having the courage to be yourself despite the internal and external pressures telling you otherwise.

Good Dress Sense

Miranda's continual throwing of her coat and accessories onto Andy Sachs' desk might be visually funny, but it smacks of someone trying to impose their identity on others, and this is at the heart of Andy's trials in the film.

In the Old Testament, shepherd boy David stepped up to the plate to fight Goliath. King Saul's response was to throw his armour and accessories across David's desk, as it were. The idea that a suit of armour made for man "head and shoulders above the rest" could fit a teenager would be amusing, if it were not so tragic.[67] The need to be true to the 'you' God intended is vital, for the secret of living in heaven's victory is to know who we are and what we have through our relationship with Jesus Christ. To allow others to impose their version of us on us undervalues what the divine weaver intended when shaping us in our mother's womb.

In a way, Saul's actions highlighted his own *insecurity*. By attempting to stamp his authority on the situation, impose his personal preference and squash any sense of originality, Saul was mirroring the behaviour of Miranda Priestley. Saul's armour and accessories were somewhat representative of himself. Although outwardly he looked *impressive*,[68] inwardly he felt *insignificant*.[69] Dominated by public opinion and believing he didn't measure up,[70] Saul "feared the people and obeyed their voice" rather than God's.[71] The king's behaviour sent the signal that he thought God had in some way made a mistake in choosing him. Eventually, this ill-adjusted attitude would rob him of his place in the world.[72]

For a divinely confident young man to take on the facade of a weak, fearful, small-minded king didn't make good dress sense.

---

67. 1 Samuel 17.
68. 1 Samuel 9:2, NIV.
69. 1 Samuel 15:17.
70. 1 Samuel 9:21.
71. 1 Samuel 15:24, ESV.
72. 1 Kings 11:11; 1 Samuel 13:14.

David needed to be true to himself. And there's a lesson for us in that. The reality is, we are not what we wear; we are what we think. "For as a man thinks within himself, so he is."[73] As the reality of this begins to dawn on Andy Sachs, she refuses to allow other people's perceptions to define her. In this she echoes the words of the Apostle Paul who, refusing to let his past define him, writes, "By the grace of God I am what I am."[74]

When we are young, we spend our time trying to figure out who we are. While some allow other people to mould their identity, others let the past define who they are. By accepting an alternative view of who we are, we risk becoming a facsimile of our true self and robbing the world of the authentic 'us'. Putting on a facade might earn the applause of others, but it will drown out the words of acceptance spoken by a loving Heavenly Father.

In *The Devil Wears Prada*, Miranda is constantly trying to shape and define Andy's identity. Miranda is arrogant, impossibly demanding and somewhat obnoxious, while Andy is uncertain, loveable, yet easily led. Desperate to discover her true self and fulfil her dream, Andy gets side-lined by her overbearing employer. However, while her boss is a force to be reckoned with, Andy Sachs is no shrinking violet either. In time, Andy will realise that she has 'sold her soul' to the vision and values of her employer and the company. Breaking the mould into which others want to squeeze her, she eventually walks away to pursue her own dream.

The Devil Wears Prada can accordingly be used as a lesson about breaking free from those internal and external pressures that seek to stop us becoming the person God intends us to be. It is about silencing the voice of intimidation, valuing our unique individuality and conquering that craving for approval that can become so addictive.

---

73. Proverbs 23:7, NASB.
74. 1 Corinthians 15:10.

The Conformity Police

To be disillusioned you first must have an illusion. The illusory world that Miranda creates for Andy is one in which you can pursue and attain satisfaction through being what you are not. This is what begins to dawn on Andy. She realises that being Miranda's personal whipping girl is a price not worth paying in the pursuit of a dream. Andy is not prepared to live a life that lacks authenticity, a life in which she becomes a copy rather than the original God intended, so she steps away from this toxic environment of conformity and compromise.

In a culture where there's no room for diversity or difference, the so-called 'Clackers' – known for the clacking noise their stiletto heels make against the marble floors – are all forced to conform to the Miranda Priestly code of practice. Crazy! Well, not really. All social groups have their own version of 'The Conformity Police'. Fearful of change and playing on the basic human need for acceptance, those in positions of authority often feel duty bound to quash any hint of self-expression. By policing the beliefs and behaviours of group members in organisations, their heavy-handedly methods help to maintain the status quo among the ordinary rank and file. This in turn creates an environment in which the entrepreneurial spirit is starved of the oxygen needed to create new ideas.

With a policy of one-size-fits-all, any corporate enterprises, be it secular or spiritual, soon becomes the dinosaur of yesteryear as difference and the celebration of diversity becomes an extinct Dodo.

When the unique 'you' is overwhelmed by manmade moulds to which you are forced to conform in order to find acceptance, then you must break free of the game which others have created.

With the growing realisation that she does not need people, prominence or possessions to validate her worth, Andy prepares to leave. Miranda, however, is adamant and dismissive. She tells her not to be silly; everyone wants to be like them.

Gird your Loins!

"Why don't chickens fly?" Why is it that a bird with wings and feathers can only manage a short, low-level flight? A chicken's dismal attempt to take to the air is the result of the oldest form of genetic engineering – selective breeding. This modern bird has been bred for food rather than flight, making its body and wing ratio unable to sustain high-level, long distant flying.

Chickens, like humans, are products of their past and illustrate the reason why we often scratch around at ground level rather than soar to our full potential. As "partakers of the divine nature", we are destined to fly like eagles rather than flap like chickens.[75] But failure to fly is often rooted in our past education, experience or environment.

Growing up in an environment that emphasises an authoritarian God to whom we will one day be answerable, rather than a loving Heavenly Father who loves us for who we are not what we do, can damage us. It can root our approval in human activity rather than heavenly acceptance. Unresolved, this can create a belief that an authority figure is our ultimate source of personal approval. In this way, submission to a parent, teacher, pastor or employer becomes our Achilles Heel – a weakness that the enemy will plunder.

How strange that midway through a 20th Century Fox movie, an ancient biblical phrase should echo around the corridors of a high-rise New York office block. Those familiar with the Old Testament will be somewhat bemused by the

---

75. 2 Peter 1:4.

phrase, "Gird your loins." It's a call to action, a battle cry. In biblical times, men and women wore long flowing garments. Although ideal for keeping cool, they were totally impractical for either hard work or battle. So, when called on, men would lift the hem of their garment and tuck it into their belt. Thus, the phrase became synonymous with a battle cry, a shout to ready oneself for confrontation – a fitting phrase when used by Nigel to forewarn the employees that Miranda Priestly was in the building!

Perhaps the New Testament parallel is "prepare your minds for action", or more literally, "gird up the loins of your mind".[76] Human loins speak of humanity's reproductive power and the ability to "reproduce after like kind".[77] In light of this, we begin to understand the power of the human mind. Not only is it the seedbed of ideas, it is also often the source of our problem. Therefore, to prepare ourselves for inevitable confrontation, we need to gather up those destructive thoughts with the "belt of God's truth".[78] By getting to grip with our thoughts we become "transformed by the renewal of (our) mind", because our *beliefs* affect our *behaviour* and ultimately whether or not we *become* the person God intended us to be.[79]

Insecurity is a fear rooted in unbelief and fed by ignorance and uncertainty.

A giant of gargantuan proportion, it dwarfs our sense of self-worth and personal ability. This Goliath can only be destroyed by the Davidic attitude that places its trust in a sovereign and all-sufficient God. In today's world, as in every era, this is an

---

76. 1 Peter 1:13, KJV.
77. Genesis 5:3, KJV.
78. Ephesians 6:14.
79. Romans 12:1-2.

antidote only appropriated through an intimate relationship with Jesus Christ and his revealed truth.

The problem of insecurity is bigger than we may think. Even politicians and popstars often struggle with the belief that they just don't measure up and don't fit in. We live in a 'Cinderella Culture' that allows the ugly sister of ignorance and uncertainty to lock us into basement thinking rather than high-level living. This is sad; God's intention is that, through a personal relationship with Jesus Christ, we head for the Ball – to a party as adopted sons and daughters, as opposed to a wake for abandoned orphans.

The real identity of a person can often be cloaked. Andy Sachs may have worn the finest clothes the fashion industry could offer, but they only served to mask her true self. When Saul put his cloak and armour on David,[80] David refused to accept it and in doing so he resisted the temptation to take on the identity of someone else to defeat Goliath. Being true to himself, David placed his trust in the fact that God's was the only approval he needed.

When the applause of men becomes more important than the approval of God, we are in danger of becoming a performance-orientated player. Life becomes a stage and our personalities are reduced to the masks that actors wear.

And this is where hypocrisy thrives.

Jesus reserved his sternest words of judgement for those who pretended to be one thing in the public domain but were something altogether in the private sphere. This kind of integrity gap provoked the harshest rebukes from him. With the Pharisees, he engaged in heated arguments, telling them that they were white-washed sepulchres – all prim and proper on the outside, but no better than a dead man's bones on the inside.

---

80. 1 Samuel 17:38.

If that wasn't bad enough, he also went onto call them a brood of vipers – all dressed up on the outside but on the inside no better than reptiles. It's hard to imagine anything worse for a religious community than being compared with a nest of creeping, crawling, conniving serpents, especially when you recall that the devil manifested as a snake in the Garden of Eden and is referred to in the Bible as that Ancient Serpent.

But there is something worse.

Jesus told these religious leaders that they were *hypocrites* – a Greek word used for those on the stage who wore masks in the theatre in ancient stage productions. Jesus was basically calling these men a bunch of actors. In our world, we'd call them 'fake'.

In the play of life, a person who is one thing in public but another thing in private is an 'actor'.

This 'actor' will play a different person on stage from the one they play off stage. Life, for them, is regarded as a performance. While the real person is who they are when they are alone, in public they present an image that will earn the audience's applause. Fearful that others will not approve of their real face, they wear a mask and become experts in the art of disguise. All the while, they work *for* approval, rather than *from* approval.

Cast of Characters

Of course, in *The Reel Story* we are talking about movies, so there really couldn't be a more apt metaphor than the Hypocrite in the original sense, the Mask-Wearing Actor. Films are the modern equivalent of ancient plays. Films, like art in general, imitate life.

In the play of life, we see a cluster of characters that time and again perform the same roles in stories of approval addiction. As they perform their various roles, keep in mind that they each demonstrate a learnt behaviour that probably began in childhood. Through some traumatic experience that has left them in a constant state of feeling vulnerable, each one has, in varying measures, become addicted to the approval of others. In these common stories, I have discovered seven, character archetypes:

- *Mr. Control Freak* – The performance of Miranda Priestly is that of a Control Freak, the person who asks all the questions and gives all the answers. When sitting in the company of a Control Freak you will be unable to get a word in edgeways. They will manipulate people and procedures in an overbearing manner. They do not listen to or value other people's contributions. Their motto is "I must be right". They dare not lose control nor allow others into the spotlight. They can never be seen to be wrong in case it exposes them as a fraud. Dominating to the point of being abusive, they bluff, badger or barrage their way through meetings and staff using exaggerated statements and out-and-out lies.

Miranda Priestly can be sardonic in the extreme. She sarcastically tells others that it thrills her when they move at the speed of a glacier. On another occasion she asks someone whether they've fallen over on the pavement and smacked their head. The Control Freak can be highly cynical and critical if it suits their goal of keeping a grip. Demeaning and disrespectful, the language of the Control Freak is rarely encouraging.

- **Mr. Know-it-all** – There are two sides to this character. There is the 'Knower' where knowledge is king. Possessing an overpowering need to be the fount of all knowledge, their seeming expertise masks their poor self-worth. Challenge their version of truth and you run the risk of triggering an explosive response. Being seen to be right, even when wrong, helps to raise their lowered sense of self-esteem.

The flipside to the 'Knower' is the 'Informer'. An insecure person will go to extreme measures to gain acceptance, even placing others in the frame, even friends, if ultimately it means gaining the approval of those in positions of power. Sharing tasty morsels of information – sometimes shared in confidence – these unscrupulous individuals use truth and untruth as a means of gaining acknowledgement.

All groups should be aware of the *insecure Informer*; they will do whatever it takes to create a momentary sense of self-worth. Having listened to and learnt from insiders, Informers stockpile information to be used as high status currency in future conversations. Knowing what others do not know is priceless ammunition in the fight to elevate their position while seeking to impress others with their worth. The journey from Informer to gossip is a short one.

Beware of the insecure, because knowledge is power. Acquiring information legitimately or illegitimately, they will wield it to gain acceptance.

If personal gain can be achieved through their information, Mr. or Mrs. Know-it-all will use it every time.

- *Mr. Angry & Argumentative* – For the insecure, domination is the name of the game. Angry at being used or abused in the past, they are easily agitated and should be labelled 'Highly Inflammable, Handle with Care'. Those working or living close to them can, through no fault of their own, spark an argument in them because they are reactors more than responders.

Reactors come in two guises. There are normal reactors that offer little resistance and then there are nuclear reactors that possess immense destructive power. I've worked with them both. I've been in meetings where people are paralysed with fear that the chairman, nicknamed Vesuvius, might at any moment erupt. I've watched out-of-the-box thinkers sit silently for fear of being frozen out, even losing their job. When deeply insecure reactors lead, fearful and frustrated staff will eventually find alternative employment – an environment in which their potential is realised and released to a greater level.

Having been in the room with this character, and witnessed their outbursts, it is not a pretty sight. Using volume to validate their point, they silence a room and create a culture in which few will be willing to share their opinion lest it triggers a negative reaction. When this character explodes, things get messy and picking up the pieces of broken relationships can take a long time. They may win individual battles, but they will most certainly lose the war.

- *Mr. Strong Silent Type* – Insecure people love silence almost as much as they like isolation. Appearing as someone knowledgeable and a valued member of the group, this character hides their ignorance behind an interested look and the occasional nod of the head in agreement, looking profound. They hide their fear of being called out on an important issue about which they have no valid input whatsoever.

Related is the 'Weak-Wordy' person. They hide their feelings of vulnerability by machine-gunning a conversation with words that leave everyone stunned. While some might be impressed, the more intuitive realise they have no idea what they are talking about.

- *Mr. Perfectionist* – Wanting to be 'practically perfect in every way', this character is the villain of the cast. Working hard to gain the applause of man rather than improve their relationship with God, he or she is overly sensitive to any constructive input. Their problem is that they have lost sight of the difference between perfectionism and the positive pursuit of excellence. Bordering on the obsessive-compulsive, the perfectionist fights a deep-seated need to correct people, objects and events. Highly critical of others, they will do whatever it takes to avoid criticism themselves. Whether adjusting a crooked picture or verbally correcting an ill-adjusted person or event, the perfectionist seeks to police everyone and everything.

Those who strive for perfection set unrealistic goals for both the perfectionist and those closely associated with them. While they might earn the accolades of others, their behaviour is a guise to silence the critical voices that might further lower their low self-esteem.

- *Mr. Pity-me-Party* – Touting for popularity with the group, the 'look-at-me-everything-is-going-wrong' character looks for approval through the pity of others. Never the life and soul of the party, they have organised their own version of events in which they are the centre of everyone's concern. This attention-getter finds a sense of worth and value in hearing other people say things like, "There, there! Never mind." Going for the 'sympathy vote', they play the crowd so that the pity of others boosts their lack of self-worth and esteem.

In the Parable of the Prodigal Son, rather than attending the party to celebrate his young brother's return, the older brother enters his own pity party. This selfish refusal to rejoice with the good fortune of others is often the behaviour of this character.

- *Mr. Worrier – and his twin brother Mr. Anxiety* – This character is more your perpetual than occasional worrier. They worry about having nothing to worry about. When their childhood lacks the necessary sense of security, an overly anxious adult is often the outcome. Chronic worriers can feel ill at ease for no reason. Often disproportionate to the person, object or event they face, the worrier displays immaturity; he or she is unable to handle the challenges of everyday life. With or without any external threat, the worrier is likely to become frozen by what might or might not happen to them or their loved ones.

Mirror Dynamics

I can so identify with Andy Sachs in her role as Miranda Priestly's personal whipping girl. In fifty years of work life, I have partnered with some delightful as well as extremely difficult individuals. While some modelled a quiet confidence emanating from the knowledge of who they were, others have manifested abusive behaviour. While the secure create a fun environment, the threatened bring an air of tension, an atmosphere in which people tiptoe around in fear.

I can think of several leaders who made my work hell, the effects spilling over into my home life. From their sudden change of direction to their lack of anger management, insecure leaders are dysfunctional guides. Maybe it was the skills of others that highlighted their weaknesses, or their inability to stick with the plan or follow a process. Staff recruitment was nothing more than a revolving door of people coming and going.

The insecure leader rarely drops their guard and employs the silent treatment or isolation punishment to maintain their position of superiority. Hiding behind a title, they blame their temper tantrums on tiredness. Continually boasting of a busy work schedule, they do whatever it takes to garner the accolades and approval of others, no matter how shallow. Like Miranda Priestly, they can lurch from the Perfectionist to the Power Freak in moments.

When sensing their position is under threat, the insecure leader will either go on the offensive or become defensive. In either case, the picture is not pretty. The veins on their head become enlarged, their face becomes red and a verbal attack takes place on the person who dares to voice a different viewpoint. I have sat in staff meetings in which no one dares offer an opinion, just in case the leader takes it wrongly.

Insecure leaders produce insecure people.

The approval addict hates this atmosphere because they need constant stroking not verbal slapping. They need personal validation from their partners and peers. They need a drip-feed of words of affirmation otherwise they are liable to 'take-their-bat-home' and refuse to play the game. The symptoms of the insecure leader can range from *Armed Warrior* to *Raging Bull*. These can make the working day a mixture of the bullring and the battlefield for the person addicted to affirmation, approval and applause.

From politicians to sports personalities and pop idols, insecurity is no respecter of persons. And in case you are wondering where my knowledge of this debilitating disease comes from, "My name is Chris Spicer and I suffer from insecurity!" I learnt it from a very young age, as many others do, growing up in an environment in which they felt they just didn't measure up to the standards set by other people.

How is it I know so much about these sad roles that I've just described? Partly because I've taken on many of these roles myself, and partly because throughout my working career, I've had the misfortune to work alongside some of the most insecure people on the planet and at times found it extremely difficult to refuse their abusive advances.

The Necessary No

If there is one word the insecure stumbles over, it's 'no'! Bound by a need to please, the sufferer feels compelled to say 'yes' to things they know they shouldn't. Even when they are maxed out and one more 'yes' could be the tipping point the fear of rejection affects their judgement.

> **Feeling vulnerable in the presence of an authority figure, the essential 'yes' overrides the necessary 'no'.**

If for no other reason than our own self-preservation, we must find a fresh grace to implement 'The Necessary No'!

Does the respectful 'no' contain such a negative connotation that its use has become unfashionable or inappropriate? When observing some well-meaning parents being unable to refuse their children's incessant asking and watching their failure to correct their children's irresponsible behaviour, I do wonder. When a disrespected employee working for an overpowering manager fears the ramifications of respectfully refusing their unfair demands, I do wonder. Have we removed the 'no' word from our verbal currency for fear of bankrupting those relationships within our sphere of influence? When people and events make the insecure feel vulnerable 'The Incessant Yes', rather than 'The Necessary No', will become the harbinger of hope that will feed their insatiable hunger for self-worth.

Secure in the knowledge of who he was, Jesus refused to bow to people-pressure. When pushed to visit sick Lazarus, seeing a bigger picture, he delayed his trip. When surrounded by a raging storm and a panicked team, Jesus rested in the knowledge that his spoken word would be accomplished.[81] Knowing how and when to use 'The Necessary No', Jesus chose to be a *Father Pleaser* rather than a *self-pleaser* or *man pleaser.*

To implement 'The Necessary No' is not easy. Some people will be confused, annoyed, disappointed or upset, but secure in the knowledge of who we are and what we are not, we should find a measure of godly confidence to lovingly, graciously and respectfully use 'The Necessary No'.

Conquering insecurity is a work of God's grace. It is dependent on us being daily enhanced and strengthened by an intimate relationship with our loving, Heavenly Father. From this foundation of knowing the Father's affection, we must set clear boundaries and find a workable mechanism for resisting intimidation. If we first find value from who we are in Christ, not from what we do, we then need an effective strategy to resist self-doubt. We must daily rejoice in our sonship rather than our successes because success is transient and elusive. Failure is a more common friend. To have a regular diet of reading and appropriating God's Word is also essential. We need more than subjective experiences of approval. We need the objective and eternal declarations of heaven, that the God of the universe – our perfect Father – rejoices over us with singing and declares that we are his much-loved sons and daughters, the pride of his life, the apple of his eye. This fusion of a firm foundation in the Father's love, with practical strategies for dealing with others' disapproval, is the key to our security.

The Goliath-like giant of insecurity can leave us feeling inadequate, unsure and doubting our ability to do what life

---

81. Luke 8:22; Isaiah 55:11

demands. But with God's help we do not have to be victims of our feelings, but victors through our freedom in Christ.

Certain of the Father's love, we no longer need to work *for* approval; we can work *from* approval.

We can learn to rest in the Father's embrace and work *from* that rest, rather than striving *for* that rest. This is always what the Father wanted for us, to enter an ongoing sabbath rest in which we know – before we say or do anything for Him – that we are greatly loved, and that heaven thinks highly of us. Jesus invited us into this rest, the rest of knowing that we are Papa's happy thought. This is the opposite of the striving and slavery of the Pharisees, who imposed a heavy load on people, giving them endless laws and regulations to obey.

Theirs was a love of law.

His was the law of love.

So, hear the invitation of Jesus again today, this time in the late Eugene Petersen's *Message* version. Hear it and rejoice. You too can break free of the Mirandas, like Andy, and find your security in the serenity of knowing who you are (identity) and fulfilling your God-given dream (destiny).

As Jesus said, "Are you tired? Worn out? Burnt out on religion? Come to me. Get away with me and you'll recover your life. I'll show you how to take a real rest. Walk with me and work with me – watch how I do it. Learn the unforced rhythms of grace. I won't lay anything heavy or ill-fitting on you. Keep company with me and you'll learn to live freely and lightly."[82]

---

82. Matthew 11:28-30, MSG.

KEEPING IT REEL

Mistakes I Have Made:
- Pretending to be what I'm not.
- Bullying others into my way of doing things.
- Allowing perfectionism to push people away.
- Being hyper-cynical and critical.
- Bowing to pressure to say 'yes'.

Lessons I Have Learnt:
- I am free to be myself.
- Finding value in 'who I am' not 'what I do'.
- I am an heir not an orphan.
- Walk in the knowledge of the Father heart of God.
- Learning 'The Necessary No'.

CHAPTER

TRAILER

Shawshank Redemption (1994) has been consistently voted many viewers' favourite film of all time. Directed by Frank Darabont and based on a story by Stephen King, it tells the story of banker Andy Dufresne (Tim Robbins) – described as an honest man and straight as an arrow – who is wrongly accused, charged and convicted of a crime and then sent to the Shawshank State Penitentiary for life. As a victim of the terrible abuse of judicial and institutional authority and power, Andy has every justification for developing a negative and hopeless attitude. But he doesn't. Instead of getting busy dying (i.e. becoming institutionalised), he gets busy living (i.e. planning his escape). He befriends a fellow inmate, an older man called Red (Morgan Freeman) and he devises a plan not only to recover his freedom, but all that has been stolen from him. After nineteen years of imprisonment, he does just that. Andy therefore represents a figure of hope for all those who are victims of the misuse and abuse of power, including within religious contexts. With the right, positive attitude, you can experience your own prison break, escape from and even subvert abusive authority, and find your way to a warm place where your memories don't hurt you anymore.

GETTING BUSY LIVING

Shawshank Redemption

The Oscar-nominated film *Shawshank Redemption* is a story about the abuse of authority, about courage in the face of injustice, and about friendship, community and brotherhood. Its hero, Andy Dufresne (Tim Robbins), is sent to prison, charged with two murders he didn't commit. Once inside, he is abused by a group of men in the showers (known as 'the Sisters'), as well as by Warden Samuel Norton, who imposes on Andy and all the other prisoners a strict combination of Bible bashing and harsh discipline. As Andy slowly fulfils his sentence, he befriends Red (Morgan Freeman), an older, African American man who becomes a mentor. This interracial camaraderie between Andy and Red is one of the most memorable friendships in cinema history. With Red's help, Andy begins to learn the ropes and develop his survival skills. This includes utilising his work experience from his life before prison and doing the accounts for the prison guards and, ultimately, for Warden Samuels. These men in authority are quite happy to use Andy's considerable gifts for their own ends. Ultimately, this blinds them to what Andy is truly doing, preparing his escape from Shawshank Prison. Andy's breakout includes crawling through a pipe filled with human excrement, but once he is free, he finds his way to a beach in Mexico where, in one of the most moving film scenes of all time, Red eventually joins him, having been released by the parole board, and broken his parole.

This story has many resonances for my wife Tina and me. We too know what it feels like to be oppressed and abused by people in authority. We too know what it feels like for people in authority to use our gifts to further their own ambitions. We too know what it's like to be in a strict regime characterised by the oppressive and controlling use of Scripture and overly harsh and indeed humiliating discipline. We too know what it's like to have your freedoms restricted and even removed, to the extent that you'll do anything it takes to escape and recapture a sense of hope. We too know what it's like to find healing and restoration in a new and faraway location after breaking out of a place of oppression. Today, Tina and I are, like Andy and Red, enjoying a new lease of life and creativity. But it hasn't always been like this. Let me tell you the story.

The Abuse of Power

In the early eighties, Tina and I, along with three children moved to the north of England – a decision my father uncharacteristically disapproved of. Posted to Manchester and Scotland in the war, anything north of Birmingham was to Dad a bad choice. But this move was to join a church with links to an international religious organisation. Without any job prospects, all we had was a borrowed deposit and a mortgage on a four-storey, stone-built, end-terrace property. For the following eight years, I worked as a self-employed carpenter while building new friendships in a local Charismatic church. I would lead a home group, then in time become an elder and eventually the senior leader of a church with around 150 adults and 100 children. That church became a vibrant community of people from all walks of life, from a garbage man to the CEO of the largest greeting card company in the UK. We were truly a multicultural and multiracial body.

In those days, the presence of God was very tangible and "all who believed were together and had all things in common"[83].

---

83. Acts 2:44.

This was a genuine move of God and I was thrilled to be a part of it. We experienced the true meaning of words like Kingdom, Community, Restoration and Church.

My twelve years with this Charismatic Christian stream in the UK taught me so much, for which I give God thanks.

Even now I would have to say that this season in our spiritual journey has wrecked us for anything less.

Then, in 1989, I accepted an invitation to take on the role of principal of the organisation's Bible College, a position that gave me greater access and insight into the workings of the overall leaders of the movement. This was a privileged and promising role; from this college, future leaders were sent out to the four corners of the world. However, this was the beginning of the end for me. My ideas about the biblical use of spiritual authority and local church autonomy were causing, if only in my own mind, an ever-increasing rift with the senior leadership of the organisation.

From my vantage point, working out of the head office, I was seeing the abuse of power. If spiritual abuse involves people assuming almost divine positions of authority, and then using coercion and control within a religious context, then that is exactly what I not only witnessed, but also what Tina and I experienced. To be frank, the reason why *Shawshank Redemption* made the final cut of this book is not only because it tells a beautiful and moving story, but also because it so poignantly and perfectly illustrates one of the most painful seasons of my life. In what follows, I will not mention any people by name. I will simply refer to the founder of the movement and his brother. I do this so as not to dishonour them. At the same time, I am keen to provide a warning against spiritual abuse in all its forms.

When men become like God to us, we encourage the abuse of power.

A New Wineskin

With the decline in denominational churches, the founder, along with his brother and others, believed that God was calling him to establish a new wineskin to contain the new wine of God's Holy Spirit being poured out in a season of spiritual renewal that was sweeping the country. These churches would be outside the well-established denominations in which most Christians found themselves. The founder never accepted that these denominations were part of God's plan and believed that God had no wish to renew and support them.

In time, the founder established a large city church and a hugely successful Bible week that drew people from all corners of the Christian Church. This annual platform was used to present the dream of a new kind of church. Using the biblical account of Israel leaving Egypt for the Promised Land, the founder, and those who stood with him, unashamedly called on those linked with a denomination to "come with us and we will do you good".[84] In this way, they urged people to leave churches and join the growing ranks of a new network of churches.

The originators of this movement undoubtedly had a passion for the Church. In an age when people were either tolerating, loathing or making fun of the Church, he longed to see local churches restored to what God initially intended.

---

84. Numbers 10:29, NASB.

In his twenties, he had caught a vision of churches fashioned after those we see in the New Testament – communities led by the Holy Spirit, unfettered by restrictive and lifeless traditions with little or no foundations in Scripture. Only these sorts of local churches would be fit to host the presence of God. Only communities like these would be drenched in the rain from heaven, namely the fresh outpouring of the Holy Spirit in our times. They alone would have the capacity to receive and maintain revival power.

A charismatic communicator, the founder was an extravagant artist who used the medium of words to paint a theological picture in which you soon found yourself personally involved. With his storytelling expertise, he could hold large congregations spellbound as he expounded biblical truth in his own inimitable way. In addition, convinced that the true church would never be restored without the ministries mentioned in Ephesians 4 (apostles, prophets, evangelists, pastors and teachers), he formed a team of gifted individuals where he was recognised as the father figure, or apostolic overseer.

An Abusive Culture

In the late eighties, as a part of a programme of expansion, this Charismatic movement purchased a seven-acre site with outbuildings. This purpose-built complex would house the Bible College, the television ministry, the team offices and a conference centre. Not everyone saw this move as a positive one. People had always remarked that the strength of the movement lay in its emphasis on relationships, in the fact that they had no equivalent of a denominational headquarters. Many felt uncomfortable about this centralised, governmental structure. This move to a brand new facility inadvertently made the apostolic team even more removed from their personal affiliation to any one local church.

In the end, this shift from a relational to a more hierarchical social structure seemed to further aggravate two very negative characteristics. The first was that local churches within the movement seemed to take on a 'sameness' that reflected the nature of the overseeing apostle. This in turn created a 'one-size-fits-all' approach that not only stifled the "multicoloured grace of God"[85], but restricted a leader's ability to grow in their gift.

The second negative effect was the abuse of authority. Although having little to do with the founder, the younger brother, to whom I was personally accountable, took on the role of a "harsh and hard" manager.[86] Based on a personal interpretation of Acts 14:23, the brothers saw it as a biblical mandate to set elders in a local church *for themselves*. These elders were to serve his apostolic vision and provide both human and financial resources for their projects.

If in the New Testament, spiritual 'authority' is used ultimately to *release* rather than *restrict* people and their gifts, this was not the case in this organisation. In this system, people were used for personal gain rather than individual growth. Perhaps it is this, more than any other negative feature, that caused leaders to leave either to join other networks or begin their own. All this led over time to the religious organisation becoming an oppressive rather than a liberating social system.

In short, I found myself in Shawshank.

The beginning of the end for me was during my time as principal of the Bible College when I had failed to launch a modular training programme in time for the annual Bible

---

85. 1 Peter 4:10, paraphrased.
86. Matthew 25:24, AMP.

week. Having once before witnessed an apostolic interrogation of a close friend, I had hoped and prayed that this was a one-off, but I was now the one in the dock and my vice principal was silently asked to observe. The verbal abuse by the younger brother continued for what seemed like a very long time. Any chance of explaining the delay was out of the question. The fact that I had spent the previous twelve months doing everything I could to meet the deadline went unheeded. It wasn't until I, a grown man, started to break down in tears that the barrage stopped. Looking back, I should have resigned there and then.

Why did I allow this? That's a question that many victims of spiritual abuse ask. I think we venerated these apostolic figures at a level that God never intended. We placed them on a pedestal and waited for divine utterances to fall from their lips. They were in control. As would-be spiritual fathers, they were overbearing and hard. Rarely did they encourage you for a job well done. And little did I realise that over time, this caused me to stop seeking God for direction for the local church I was leading because I had come to believe that this was handed down from those in authority. The apostle was regarded as the senior elder of every local church under their covering. Those in authority set both our personal and corporate destiny by exercising ultimate control, which looking back "made them God to us". The freedom to be the person God had called you to be was difficult; it was as if, to be accepted, you had to become a mini version of your apostle in what you thought and said.

I was in my own version of Shawshank. Andy and his fellow inmates had become 'institutionalised'. They had found themselves in a regimented establishment from which there was seemingly no escape. With a daily routine, fixed patterns of behaviour and the equalising effect of their prison uniforms, all the inmates experienced an oppressive environment. Although no one in Shawshank understood what the two ladies were singing about, for one moment everyone felt free.

That was my story too. Although never vocalised, the religious movement I joined had its own language, practices and dress code. To try and implement any changes to these codes was viewed as rebellious and divisive.

Perhaps you can see now why I wanted to do what Andy did and deafen the whole institution with my version of the opera singer, to show others what they were missing through this imposed incarceration. The piece of music in question was taken from one of Mozart's most popular operas, *The Marriage of Figaro*. Even if it had meant some form of isolation for me, the momentary joy of "every last person feeling free" would have been worth it.

Spiritual Abuse Defined

In his forward for the recent book, *Escaping the Maze of Spiritual Abuse*, by Lisa Oakley and Justin Humphreys, Mark Stibbe defines spiritual abuse. Spiritual abuse is the abuse of power in a religious context, usually in the form of manipulation and control, using divine authority and the words of Scripture to justify the restriction of freedom. Mark is himself a victim of a shocking instance of this. As I read down his list, I found myself taken back to my time in the religious organisation. Although my abuse was verbal, it was spiritual in character; God's name was evoked in me submitting to the trauma I suffered.

Coercion to Conform

When I think back, the pressure to conform to my abuser's legalistic version of Christianity was at times overwhelming. What my abuser was in public was often very different to the person who confronted me in private. A seemingly pastoral and caring man would turn into a radical tyrant, especially when he was crossed.

Exploitation

Just as Andy was exploited for what his abusers could get out of him – his time and skills were harnessed for the abuser's own ends – so I and others were exploited in much the same way. Our resources were mined by abusive leaders for self-aggrandising and empire-building purposes. This was highly dysfunctional.

Manipulation

Just as Warden Norton manipulated Bible verses to feather his own nest and further his own personal agenda, I observed the way that biblical truths about God's covenant relationship with us were being applied as a coercive and manipulative tool to keep people in their place, to stop them from making a break for freedom.

Divine Position

Spiritual abusers often undermine the core tenets of the Reformation by setting themselves up as a mediator between their victims and God, thereby reducing the effectiveness of the atonement. When my wife Tina describes our time in the religious organisation (twelve years in all), she simply concludes by saying, "They became God to us."

Enforced Accountability

In Shawshank, you could not even go to the bathroom without asking permission, such was the level of accountability. My situation was restrictive too. I felt incarcerated, sentenced to a regime of ruthless accountability. This curbed my freedom to be and become anything other than what my abuser determined.

Censorship of Decision-making

Shawshank removed the ability of its inmates to make any decision for themselves. In my story, decisions concerning our town/city of residence, the homes we bought, the company we kept and the cars we drove were all either overtly or covertly censored.

The Requirement of Secrecy and Silence

Unspoken 'gagging orders' seemed to have been enforced in my situation even before we had heard of the term. Even now, few people will speak out about the abuse they suffered. Whether through fear, or through some warped view of loyalty, few ex-participants speak out. I raise it now not for purposes of revenge, but to make sure this never happens again.

Requirement of Obedience to the Abuser

The submission required of us using Hebrews 13:17 (one of many examples of the misuse of Scripture) meant I became submerged in a sea of unquestioning obedience to my abuser. Unable to counter their requests, I became like an inmate of Shawshank. The demands of absolute obedience stifled the real me and moulded me into a 'yes sir!' person.

Isolation as a Means of Punishment

In Shawshank, the Warden's favourite word, 'solitary', pointed to his preferred means of punishment. When confronting insecure people, leaders in my context often used isolation as punishment. Whereas a loving Heavenly Father "sets the solitary in family", legalistic father figures reversed this by setting people in solitary confinement.[87]

Superiority and Elitism

The view of those outside the religious organisation was comparable to that of the two-and-a-half tribes who stayed the

---

87. 84 Psalm 68:6.

other side of Jordan. 'Come with us and we will do you good' was a popular theme to encourage those in a denominational setting to leave and join those moving in obedience to God's progressive revelation. All this betrayed an elitist, superior spirit.

Camaraderie

One redeeming factor of life in Shawshank was not only Andy's friendship with Red, but the camaraderie he enjoyed with a select group of inmates. This is not only a film about the quest for freedom and the resilience of the human spirit, it's a movie about friendship. Whether the camera is focusing on the prison yard, library, dining room or the roof, each scene demonstrates the importance of the camaraderie formed in Shawshank. Marginalised from society, a small group of inmates found security in each other's friendship.

Although from different backgrounds, with different stories of what brought them to Shawshank, this band of brothers not only stood together throughout the hardships of everyday life, they also forged a fellowship which gave each one of them a sense of belonging. Being there for each other in the good times and the bad, each inmate experienced trust and companionship, solidarity and mutual support.

For some, like the old prisoner called Brookes (who worked in the prison library), the loss of this supporting network proved too much to bear. Confronted with the prospect of losing this camaraderie, he takes drastic and desperate measures.

I empathise with Brookes.

When I left the abusive religious organisation in question, I mourned the loss of togetherness I had enjoyed with a small group of brothers. Although most came from different backgrounds to me, we had all paid a price to be together during this season. I experienced the loss of family connections. Former friends turned their back on me because I'd entered what was back then thought of as a radical group of Christians. Losing my liberty to mix with others outside of the organisation made friendship with others in the organisation even more necessary.

Just as Red missed his friend Andy following his escape, I still miss the camaraderie of that band of brothers. In all honesty, what I experienced was real friendship and it has ruined me for anything less. Living close to others strips you of all pretence; the mask falls and the 'real you' soon emerges. In that raw state, I found people who accepted, appreciated and approved of me despite my apparent weakness. They brought the best out of me.

Although I thank God for those I have served with in the subsequent years, nothing has ever matched that band of brothers and I mourn the loss of true camaraderie. We did life together. Our families shared days together. We worked on each other's homes and went on vacation together. Besides sharing a common belief, we shared a common bond that brought the best out of us.

Community

Andy and Red belonged to a small community whose glue was in part the fact that they were in prison, but mostly the fact that as people they enjoyed being together. The cohesive power of friendship, especially when those involved are in a situation of duress, should never be underestimated. Bonds are forged on the anvil of testing that often go deeper than those formed in the absence of adversity. Andy, Red and the other friends in their group created a community within the institution of Shawshank, and it was this that helped them to endure the grave restrictions to their freedoms.

In the earliest days of the Church, as recorded in the Book of Acts, a community was created in the face of persecution, including the threat of imprisonment. As early as Acts 3, Peter and John are being arrested and questioned for proclaiming the name of Jesus to others in Jerusalem. After the outpouring of the Holy Spirit on the Day of Pentecost (Acts 2), a community of over 3,000 followers of Jesus had been established after Peter had preached the Good News and many had turned to the Lord to receive salvation. By the end of Acts 2, we read that this community of believers shared everything they had. No one went without food or clothing. Everyone's needs were met, whether practical or pastoral.

This was one of the most appealing and attractive things about the religious organisation I joined in its early years. Everyone had paid a price to be there, as the followers of Jesus did when they joined the community in the Book of Acts. Speaking for myself, I considered it worthwhile, to begin with at least.

Having burnt our bridges, for many of us there was no going back.

But this didn't matter; the strong bond of community more than compensated for it.

In Andy's case, all his close friends had one thing in common: they had been locked up, whether justly or unjustly, and the shared context of incarceration, along with the need to survive, brought about the need for a smaller, more meaningful network of relationships. This was true for me in my story. It is also true more generally for the Church today. As freedoms become more and more restricted for Christians, as the host culture all around us becomes more and more secular and anti-Christian, we need to cultivate true community. We need to meet in larger gathered contexts, yes, but we also need the smaller, home-based communities of friendship as well, perhaps more so if Christians are forced to go underground, as in the persecution of the Chinese churches during the twentieth century. We will need to have learnt the importance of being dispersed, not just gathered – of being home-based, not just Temple-based. We will need to have learnt some lessons from Andy and Red!

Even after the restrictions of my own freedoms within the religious organisation, I still believe that authentic Christian community is one of the USPs (Unique Selling Points) of the Christian Church, but sadly there is little *cost* involved being a Christ-follower in our post-Christian and increasingly anti-Christian culture. The all too easy 'Come to Christ by saying the sinner's prayer' method of recent years is as far removed from New Testament Christianity as we can get. Jesus told his potential followers to count the cost before they took up their crosses to come after him, living lives of self-denial. This lack of cost has created a more casual version of Christianity, marked by compromise and consumerism not commitment, and this is the furthest remove from what the early Church experienced in the Book of Acts.

If I'm honest, I miss that sense of authentic, costly community that we had, and the camaraderie – the deep friendships – that came with it.

It's the closest thing I've experienced to the sense of community that's manifest in the Early Church in Acts 2.

I long for that again, but without all the heavy shepherding, spiritual abuse, and restrictions of freedoms that went with it.

Getting Busy Living

How do any of us ever survive these seasons of restriction? For Andy Dufresne, a positive mental attitude proved vital. Famously, he said "get busy living, or get busy dying". In other words, you can either get busy planning to have a life, planning to enjoy the glorious freedom which is your right, or you can get busy slowly dying, blending into an oppressive culture, losing your unique individuality, becoming institutionalised rather than human.

We should never underestimate the power of a positive attitude.

Viktor Frankl, who spent three years in various Nazi concentration camps, wrote: "Everything can be taken from a man but one thing: the last of the human freedoms – to choose one's attitude in any given set of circumstances, to choose one's own way."[88] Our attitude shapes our future.

---

88. Viktor E. Frankl, *Man's Search for Meaning*, Rider, 2004, p.75.

During the last stages of my time in the religious organisation, I decided to write a book about the eight beatitudes that Jesus utters in Matthew 6. These beatitudes are sometimes referred to as 'Be-attitudes' or 'Attitudes-to-be'. They are Jesus' version of "get busy living" – living life in all its superabundance in the Kingdom of God, as opposed to getting busy dying in someone else's empire, under their oppressive rule.

When I eventually told my apostle (the founder's brother) that I had fulfilled a fifteen-year dream of writing my first book (*Eight Characteristics of Highly Effective Christians*, published by Monarch), his response was very hurtful. "Was this written in your own time, or while you were being paid?" No encouragement was given at all. No congratulations for a job well done. It was very painful. Very disappointing.

When I was nearing the end of my tenure as Bible College principal, I was asked to write a paper on the New Testament view of authority. My conclusion was that God's delegated authority was ultimately designed to 'release' not 'restrict' those in our care – just as a parent exercises authority over their children ultimately to release them into society as happy and productive citizens. This paper was not received well.

How, then, did we escape? In many ways, it was decided for us in what my wife and I now refer to as 'The McDonald's Meeting'. By then, I'd been encouraged to leave my role as Bible College principal and had completed a year-long master's degree in Peace Studies at Bradford University. We had been strongly encouraged to move to Scotland by our apostle, but we did not believe this was God's destiny for us. Things quickly deteriorated from then on. We even received spurious public prophecies by one of the apostle's most faithful followers, about making wrong decisions that would "take us up a narrow channel instead of the oceans that God had destined for us".

This all came to a head when Tina and I met with the apostle in McDonalds. Here we were once again faced with our faults and failings, as well as veiled threats that we were in a place of disobedience and we would suffer the consequences of our so-called 'breaking covenant'. By this time, I had had enough and challenged the man, asking if he was threatening us, which he denied. He quickly terminated the meeting, and we quickly terminated our association with his religious organisation. The meeting ended with a business handshake rather than a brotherly hug, which probably said more than words ever could.

When I left, I left believing the lie that I was a failure.

I was hurt, offended, angry and bitter. For years afterwards, I had bad dreams that always included the apostolic figure who verbally abused me. All my life, I had felt insecure when confronted by authority figures, but this season forged a deeper sense of fear, low self-esteem and poor self-image. I would often take my frustration out on the one person who knew and loved me most, my wife Tina. This is turn brought stress in our marriage. Even today, I suffer the consequences; I do not easily give my trust to others. I often choose independence over interdependence. It's taken years to discover the Father heart of God and to appreciate that I am loved for who I am, not what I do. Like Andy, I've had to crawl through a lot of muck, but I'm a free man now.

Writing this book, especially this chapter, has proved to be very cathartic. My hope is that it will prevent others falling into the same trap. We must always resolve to let God be God and not let men replace Him.

KEEPING IT REEL

Mistakes I Have Made:

- Overstaying your welcome.
- Placing leaders on pedestals.
- Listening to men rather than listening to God.

Lessons I Have Learnt:

- Kinetics: some things keep running even when the power is turned off.
- Some leaders can be a liability to recover from not a goal to aim for.
- Insecure leaders create bland and boring churches.
- Empire-building is not of God.

CHAPTER

TRAILER

Molokai (1999) is arguably the least known movie in this book. It tells the story of a Roman Catholic priest in the nineteenth century – Father Damien – who volunteered to serve a colony of lepers on the island of Molokai. Fighting against both ecclesiastical and political authorities off the island, and the mistrust and hostility of the lepers on it, he perseveres in his mission to do what Christ did and bring the Father's love to a marginalised and despised community. In this regard, Father Damien represents the epitome of true Christian leadership. He did not seek to gain prominence and position in order to misuse power by restricting other's freedoms. Rather, he sought to serve the most neglected and abject people on the earth, not as a visible celebrity but as one of heaven's invisible, unsung heroes. 'Till his last breath, Father Damien acts as a super-servant not a superstar, bringing into sharp focus what leadership truly looks like in the Church of the future, as well as providing a therapeutic story for those who have been wounded by the Church of the past. For those in the Church who have been used to distant rather than relational leaders, to leaders wielding titles rather than towels, *Molokai* is a lasting reminder that, like Jesus, true leaders come to serve, not be served, and to give their lives for many (Mark 10:45).

SUPER-SERVANTS
AND SUPERSTARS

Molokai

Some movies have an extraordinary capacity to make us laugh, cry or scream. This became very clear to me when I was invited to a private viewing of Mel Gibson's *The Passion of the Christ* (2004). That was a cinema experience I shall neither forget nor want to repeat. The emotional impact of this movie was extreme, like watching the violent death of a loved one. As the credits rolled, people refused to leave. We sat in stunned silence as the shock and awe took hold, struggling to process what we had just experienced. No one talked. We didn't even acknowledge the presence of others in the room. The emotional impact had rendered us speechless.

I have selected the ten movies that frame *The Reel Story* because of the emotional effect each one had within the season of my life in which I first saw them. This is particularly true of the relatively unknown film, *Molokai*. While some films have *mugged* me, others have *ministered* help and healing. *Molokai* is an example of the latter.

After leaving the religious organisation mentioned in the last chapter, I felt like the victim in the Good Samaritan story – as if a gang of hooligans had attacked me and left me half dead at the roadside of life. Stripped of my identity and robbed of my dignity, I was struggling to survive.[89] Events beyond my control had overtaken me. Bruised and broken, I hoped that some kind person would have mercy on my misfortune and administer healing.

---

89. Luke 10:30.

However, at this point my story departs from the parable Jesus told. Rather than passing me by, it was a priest who became part of my road to recovery. Not a literal priest, but a character in the film *Molokai*, the hero, Father Damien.

In the late 1970s, we began to receive cassette tapes from a church in Portland, Oregon. These recordings breathed spiritual life into my wife Tina and me. In our first church leadership role, we were way out of our depth. Feeling overwhelmed and sinking fast, the radical worship and refreshing preaching on these tapes threw us a lifeline.

Having returned from our honeymoon to pioneer a church in the Northamptonshire town of Daventry, all I had learnt at Bible College now seemed gloriously irrelevant. Daventry was a town created to cater for the overspill from the UK's second city, Birmingham. As such, it had become the dumping ground for troubled families. Our small congregation was central to a new sprawling social housing complex nicknamed 'Dodge City'. It was here we were apprenticed in the joys and sorrows of church leadership. Church politics, problem people, loneliness, poverty, depression and the pressure to perform to other people's expectations became a heavy load for a young married couple.

Living on a minimum wage in social housing was way outside my middle-class comfort zone.

Tina, pregnant with our first child, was working while I travelled a forty-mile round trip to work part-time in my father's business. Times were hard and we were surviving by the grace of God and the goodness of people. This was Pastoring 101, church leadership in the raw. Living in this harrowing time, the monthly tapes from Portland became an oasis in an otherwise dry and barren existence.

Over the subsequent years, our links with Portland grew until, hearing of our plight after we had left the abusive organisation, the senior pastor, Dick Iverson, extended an invitation to us to spend 1994 in what was back then known as Bible Temple, but in time became City Bible Church, and today Mannahouse. As Good Samaritans, they took us in and cared for us, helping us to recover from our wounds in the inn of their church.

It was here, while spiritually convalescing, that I was first introduced to Father Damien and ultimately the film *Molokai*. Few of you may have heard, let alone watched, this movie. Yet the impact of its storyline in this season of my life cannot be overstated. Father Damian represented the furthest remove from the kind of spiritual leadership I had witnessed in my twelve years of abuse. This was not empire-building, unhealthy, superstar leadership. This was kingdom-building, healthy servant leadership. Watching this on screen and living it at the hands of Dick Iverson and his congregation, gave me a chance to recover from my experience of spiritual abuse, and restored my sense of what a true leader is meant to look like.

A True Christian Hero

Released in 1999, *Molokai* is based on the true story of a Belgian Roman Catholic priest called Father Damien (played by David Wenham) who serves the lepers quarantined in a colony on the Hawaiian island of Molokai. It is 1872, and Father Damien agrees to go to the lepers of Kalaupapa to minister to the sick for three months. The local area bishop has decided that priests need to live and work within the leper's settlement to administer to the inhabitants when they die. Father Damien bravely volunteers and leaves with the bishop's blessing, as well as a warning not to touch any of the lepers.

On arriving, Father Damien finds that the lepers have been herded to a remote part of the island where they are living in appalling poverty and neglect. He sets about improving their living conditions, building and repairing their huts, and helping them with their spiritual lives, urging them to turn away from the sins they are committing in order to find some comfort from their harsh existence. Father Damien also finds the local chapel in disrepair and sets about restoring it. A boy from the island volunteers to help and becomes the altar boy as services start up again. He then finds a non-Catholic Englishman, played by Peter O' Toole, who has now become a leper and is seriously ill. He had originally been a medical assistant but had caught the disease himself. Although not sympathetic to the Catholic faith, the man finds great comfort in Father Damien, who is unfazed by the fact that the patient doesn't share his convictions. When he dies, Father Damien buries his body in the Catholic cemetery.

As Father Damien sets about serving the settlement, he fights for the government to provide medicine and supplies, but these appeals fall on deaf ears. The local newspapers, however, begin to hear about what is happening and run stories highlighting the plight of the lepers and their need for assistance. Leaders in government are furious; they would much rather the lepers were forgotten altogether. Father Damien, however, will not let up in his struggle against absurd bureaucratic obstacles.

Over time, Father Damien begins to show the symptoms of leprosy and his bishop visits him. However, the bishop will only hear his confession from the safety of a boat. He will not risk catching the disease himself. As the self-sacrificial priest becomes more and more sick, he fights for the rights of the suffering lepers of Molokai until a new priest arrives, accompanied by some nuns, to assist him. These religious sisters heroically serve the lepers too.

In the end, Father Damien collapses during Mass, a true Christian hero, and is taken to his own hospital where he dies. He was declared a saint by Pope Benedict in 2009. The state of Hawaii has placed a statue of Father Damien in the statuary hall in the US Capitol.

The Opposite of Superstar Christianity

It's hard for me to put into words the emotional impact and healing power of this movie when I first saw it. The story of *Molokai* was the antithesis of all that I had experienced over the previous twelve years in terms of spiritual leadership. It not only softened my hardened heart; it also opened my eyes to the reality of what true, Christ-like, servant-hearted leadership looks like and restored my faith in the possibility of seeing it and even living it. Demonstrating great humility, Father Damien built an inclusive rather than an exclusive community, openly promoting a policy of 'no perfect people here'. He was the furthest remove from the remote, superstar leaders at whose hands I had suffered. He was, and is, a true hero.

The island of Molokai's natural beauty is incredible, yet its horrific history is incomprehensible. As the location for America's only Leper Colony, the island represents a dark chapter in US history. Forcibly taken from their homes, families and friends, men, women and children suspected of having leprosy where forcibly exiled to the island. This is reckoned to be the longest and deadliest medical segregation in US history.[90]

Between 1866 and 1969, more than 8,000 people were loaded like cattle into ships and dumped into a lawless society there. This was a place that few dared to venture for fear of being killed or contracting this highly contagious disease. Yet it was

---

90. John Taymen, *The Colony: The Harrowing True Story of Exiles of Molokai*, Simon & Schuster, 2006.

into this desperate environment that a 33-year-old Belgium priest stepped, immersing himself in the spiritual, physical and social needs of this isolated community of outcasts. Although he was only meant to be there for three months, he ended up staying sixteen years, until he too succumbed to the terrible disease and died. Having requested permission to extend his stay, Damien's Bishop confirmed that he could stay as long as his devotion allowed. Compelled by compassion, he spent the rest of his short life sharing his faith, teaching carpentry, farming, singing and engaging in sports in order to restore a sense dignity and normality to the colony. He embraced a God-given mission that would involve digging a thousand graves and walking on average ten miles a day to care for the sick and dying. He cared for his patients, built houses, schools, roads, hospitals and churches. He dressed ulcers, built coffins, shared pipes and food while providing spiritual, medical and emotional solace for those in the colony. Repeatedly warned by his superiors not to eat with or touch the people, Damien *"was moved with compassion and touched the leper"*.[91] Damien embraced the leper but not the disease.

My Road to Recovery

By the end of the 90s, when I saw this film, I was beginning to process what had happened to me during my later years in the religious organisation. Treated as a social outcast, it had been made abundantly clear that I was no longer welcome and would be well advised to get out of town. In God's economy, *"all things work together for good for those who are called according to his purpose"*.[92] When God's children are in the fiery furnace, He never leaves them alone. His investment is too valuable to allow the words and actions of unscrupulous

---

91. Mark 1:40-41 Emphasis added.
92. Romans 8:28, ESV. Emphasis added.

leaders to consume his gold. The fire will undoubtedly test us, but God's grace is great enough to remove the stench of bitterness and the scorching effects of shame. The fire will refine us not ruin us.

Having taken a year out to pursue a master's degree at university, I would eventually return to a 'tent making' role of shopfitting. This was a season of patiently waiting for God to open a door of opportunity. Throughout my life, the faithfulness of God has often transplanted me from a setting in which my God-given gifts were neither recognised nor released into a safe place in which I could become all that God intended.

In 1994, through a series of divinely orchestrated events, Tina and I, along with three of our four children, relocated to Portland, Oregon, USA. At the invitation of Pastor Dick Iverson, we would begin our journey to recovery while spending a year of spiritual convalescence in this beautiful part of the world. Selling what we could to raise the money for our airfares, we rented out our house in the UK and headed out to America.

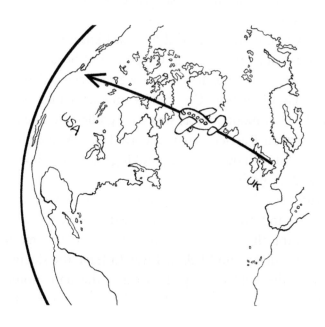

Brother Iverson proved to be an exceptional pastor. Although a busy man leading a congregation of 3,000 people, he found time to leave his granddaughter's birthday party to meet us at the airport. This was true servant leadership. Having been given what in Pastor Iverson's words was the 'gold card', we had access to all areas of church life. This was a large church with its own Bible College and day school. As our student visa dictated, Tina and I spent our mornings studying in the college, while our second eldest daughter Hannah began a theology degree. Our two boys would be educated at the day school. During the afternoons, Tina would work in a janitorial role and I worked in the maintenance department.

This turned out to be a year of emotional healing. Through much grief and brokenness, I started to discover the Father heart of God. I had spent a lifetime looking to those in authority for approval – my father, teachers, church leaders, employers. They were all authority figures to whom I looked for acceptance. All this had succeeded in doing was create an open season for my spiritual abusers.

However, the unconditional love and kindness shown to us along this short but amazing Oregon Trail began the healing process. Here, for the first time, we experienced the Father heart of God in action. Our college and school fees were paid for and accommodation, as well as a golden car the size of a Naval Aircraft Carrier, was made available. Although we had to be careful with our finances, looking back I can honestly say we lacked for nothing.

I had been hurt deeply by the bullish behaviour of one individual and my self-worth was on the brink of bankruptcy. Approaching the age of fifty, this was a half-time moment in which I needed to find help if I was to leave the sidelines and return to the field of play. This came through moments of resting in the presence of God and the pastoral care of certain kind-hearted individuals. And it came in the unexpected form of a hitherto unknown Catholic Priest.

Father Damien.

Super-servants not Superstars

Who would have thought that a movie about Catholic Priest could prove to be so cathartic, that a story about a missionary serving a colony of lepers would reboot my understanding of true Christian leadership and kickstart my road to recovery? Father Damien was a leader who refused to cower beneath those in authority who sought to override the will of God for his life. Here was a man who mirrored the ministry of Jesus, a leader who empathised with those he sacrificially served. Here was my introduction to servant-hearted leadership.

Whether because of my recent experience of abusive leadership, or because of my wounded and vulnerable state, the story of Father Damien began in me a process of inner healing. Damien's Christ-like leadership became something of an antidote to the poison I'd been infected with by others. In true priestly fashion, Father Damien "stood between the dead and the living"[93] and although the plague was not 'halted' as in Moses' day, the loss of hope, dignity and normality were diminished. Father Damien shepherded his flock of castaways in a truly God-inspired manner! In time, the story of the lepers he served became emblematic of my own need for help as a castaway.

Why has his example been so important to me? It's because Father Damien is the true embodiment of the Super-servant and the exact opposite of the Superstar. Although memorials have been erected in his memory, and sainthood bestowed on him, Father Damien was always an invisible and humble servant not a star under lights.

---

93. Numbers 16:48.

His example of servant-hearted leadership realigned my vision and restored my hope after all the spiritual abuse I endured.

Having grown up in Church, I've listened to countless stories of heroes of the faith who "knew their God and did exploits"[94] but somehow the Father Damien story was different. As I sat in that classroom listening to the teachers share principles of leadership, I was gripped by the account of this young Belgium priest who "served the purpose of God in his generation".[95] Although my respect for Christian leadership was at an all-time low, here was a man who lived his whole life outside the spotlight. His name would never be emblazoned on posters; he would never be top of a conference billing, nor would he ever be headhunted by some megachurch. Here was a true servant of God who worked with a huge community of outcasts. Fame and fortune would never be his driving force. His calling was to comfort the orphans and care for the dying. He served for the approval of one, not the applause of the many. Here was a leader who lived in line with the Beatitudes and because of that was "blessed, happy, enviably fortunate and spiritually prosperous".[96] His simple yet sublime servant life became the antithesis of what I had spent all those years observing in the religious organisation. In God's 'upside-down-kingdom' – in which the least is the greatest, the poor are rich and the last shall be first – Father Damien was more interested in building God's Kingdom than man's empire.

I remember standing in a darkened room filled with the stench of urine. This was the Urology Department of a

---

94. Daniel 11:32, KJV.
95. Acts 13:36, NASB.
96. Matthew 5, AMP.

government-run West African hospital. Through the darkness, a shadowy figure could just be seen under the shabby piece of cloth that was a patient's bedcovering. It cost around £5 or $7 to see a doctor, and half that to see a nurse.[97] Our guide told us that often people came to the hospital with one health problem and caught additional infections from which they died. Although a cluster of white-coated medical staff moved slowly from room to room, the atmosphere was dire.

The only relief we received from this tragic scene was chatting to a pastor who had, over the last thirty years, made it his life mission to comfort these patients, often giving them money to see a doctor or to purchase medicine. He told us that he had had the joy of praying for 20,000 people who wanted to know Jesus. Across the African Continent, I have met leaders like this who are 'heaven's unsung heroes'. Their names are sadly long since forgotten, but their faithful service is indelibly etched on my mind. These are not your classic Western celebrity pastors who are known for their numerous conference appearances, charismatic communication, and titled names. These were very different; they were true servants, whose silent, sacrificial dedication will one day be openly rewarded.

While the prominence of titled leaders is visible everywhere in the West, the Church today needs those, like Jesus, holding the towel of selfless service. Those who stand in the gap function in a priestly or intermediary manner![98] By taking the hand of the hurting, they seek to introduce them through acts of kindness to a loving heavenly father.

This is the ministry of the Super-servant, not the Superstar.

It is the ministry of Father Damien.

It is the ministry of Jesus.

---

97. Exchange rates in 2018.
98. Ezekiel 22:30.

Reel Therapy

During our stay in Portland, the story of Father Damien became a source of 'reel therapy'. While I'd been working in the religious organisation, an offence had been sown into the insecure ground of my innermost being. Left unattended, it would have grown into a root of bitterness and produced the fruit of resentment. I needed an environment in which to resolve these issues and this inspiring story, along with the example of the church leaders in Portland, began the process of healing my hurts and hang-ups.

What I came to see was that Father Damien was a leader who embraced people rather than distancing himself from them. I had witnessed leaders keeping themselves at arm's length, sitting in ivory towers whose foundations had become faulty and whose walls were crumbling. Damien was the opposite to this. Although being told repeatedly not to touch the island residents, he went out of his way to embrace those with leprosy. Like the Christ he served, he "was moved with compassion [and] touched the leper".[99] Here was a level of empathy I had not seen before. It became an antidote to the venom in my spiritual veins.

This man of God worked tirelessly to restore dignity to those he served. Rather than withholding what he had in a controlling manner, he operated an open-hand policy.

All that he had he made available for the help and healing of others.

Here was a man who preferred to be selfless rather than selfish. Here was a man who refused to be a consumer of other's gifts but chose rather to be consumed by the purpose

---

99. Mark 1:41.

of God for his life. Here was a servant leader who knew that "a commitment to God is a call to inconvenience that will ruin your ambitions and play havoc with your privacy".[100] He had no interest in competing with others; he was only interested in completing his race. He had the committed heart of a mature son, not the competitive heart of an unhealed orphan.

Where did this competitive spirit come from that pervades so much of Church life? Why do leaders classify fellow leaders by the size of their congregation? If only we could see ourselves as Father Damien did – as runners in our individual lanes *completing* our race rather than *competing* against other Christ-followers, so that in time we can say with the Apostle Paul, "I have finished [*my*] race."[101]

Put another way, it's time to take down the ladder, to dismantle the secular idea of climbing the ladder of success. There should be no system of promotion in the Kingdom of God in which those with more responsibility are regarded as having a higher value. When we do this, we create a ranking system that results in a 'see you at the top' mentality. Those on the 'lower rungs' get stepped on and regarded as irrelevant. "For promotion cometh neither from the east, nor the west, nor from the south. It is God who judges: He brings one down, He exalts another. Promotion or exaltation comes from God."[102] As Henri Nouwen writes, "When we start being too impressed by the results of our work, we slowly come to the erroneous conviction that life is one large scoreboard where someone is listing the point to measure our worth. And before we are fully aware of it, we have sold our soul to the many grade-givers. That means we are not only in the world, but also of the world. Then we become what the world makes of us."[103]

---

100. Charles Simpson, "Commitment to God & His People." New Wine Magazine, June 1978, 10.6, Christian Growth Ministries.
101. 2 Timothy 4:7. Emphasis added.
102. Psalm 75:6–7.
103. Henri J. M. Nouwen, *Out of Solitude: Three Meditations on the Christian Life*, Ave Maria Press, p.22.

Perhaps it's time to turn the pyramid upside down so that leaders are at the bottom, cheering and supporting others to reach their destiny.

Being "servant leaders"[104] in the true sense of the word means that we are 'under-rowers' – leaders who work hard in the bowels of the boat, propelling others to their destination, not captains of all they survey.

Christianity fosters its fair share of superstars, those whose popularity seems as impressive as their prominence. Often imitated but never duplicated, so-called superstars are high-profile, talented, extremely charismatic individuals who become those pinnacle people to whom so many look up. Humanity seems to hanker after such celebrities. Instead of looking to the Light of the World, they too readily turn instead to shining lights for guidance, while at the same time trying to emulate their actions, appearance and attitude to life.

The 1970s rock opera *Jesus Christ Superstar* may have portrayed Jesus as a Superstar, but the truth is he was a Super-servant. He was always redirecting the glory and praise away from himself and towards his Father. He described kingdom greatness as being subservient rather than being superior. Discussing true greatness, he made this declaration:

"For who is the greater, one who reclines at table or one who serves? Is it not the one who reclines at table? But I am among you as the one who serves."[105]

There are far too many in the Church today seeking titles rather than towels. Jesus laid aside his outer garment and picked up a towel to serve others by washing their feet – a task

---

104. 1 Corinthians 4:1–2, NASB.
105. Luke 22:27, ESV.

that even the most menial slave in his day was not required to do. Here is true servant leadership; we should never forget that, speaking about exercising authority as a leader, Jesus said, "I am among you as one who serves."[106]

In the movie *Molokai*, I see the essence of true leadership in which a man with authority is also under authority.[107] As I made my first initial steps to recovery, Father Damien, though dead, left his mark on my life, showing me what the new leadership in the Church should really look like. The old wineskin of a charismatic individual leading a company, church or charitable organisation is changing. The entrepreneurial leader that people looked and longed for is fast becoming something of the past. Too many have taken the term 'apostle' and made it synonymous with control, charisma and forceful personalities who impose their will on others, restricting rather than releasing God's potential in others. Without authentic spiritual fathers and mothers, the Church becomes a firm not a family, where managers focus on creating a culture of earning value through performance. May God help us to be Super-servants rather than hankering after becoming Superstars.

Speaking personally, I have Father Damien to thank for helping me to see and embrace this paradigm shift from Superstar to Super-servant.

And I have the movie *Molokai* to thank for giving me a picture of what this new leadership – which is as old as Jesus himself – truly looks like.

---

106. Ibid.
107. Matthew 8:5–13.

KEEPING IT REEL

Mistakes I Have Made:

- Allowing the root of bitterness to produce the fruit of resentment.

- Not celebrating the wins with our children.

- Misunderstanding the difference between isolation and insulation.

- Giving up instead of giving in.

- Believing I was a loser who sometimes wins and not a winner who sometimes loses.

Lessons I Have Learnt:

- Failure is not final.

- Charismatic leadership is often a liability to recover from more than a goal to aim for.

- God insulates not isolates us from the world.

- A commitment to God will plunder your ambitions and play havoc with your privacy.

- God's timings are perfect.

CHAPTER

TRAILER

What About Bob? (1991) is a dark comedy about the relationship between a psychiatrist called Dr Leo Marvin (Richard Dreyfuss) and a patient called Bob Wiley (Bill Murray). When Bob's regular psychiatrist has had enough of him, he palms Bob off onto Dr Marvin, author of a new book – *Baby Steps* – that's attracting a great deal of media attention, much to the doctor's delight. As Bob comes into his world, however, Dr Marvin's patience and expertise are challenged. Bob, a sufferer from multiple phobias, is recovering from a divorce brought about by the chasmic differences between himself and his ex-wife. When Dr Marvin goes on his much-anticipated, month-long vacation, Bob can't cope. The doctor tells Bob to take a vacation from his problems, but Bob decides instead to take a vacation to where the doctor is staying. As the doctor tries maintain boundaries, Bob becomes more and more popular with Marvin's wife and two children – both named after two famous psychiatrists, Anna and Sigmund. They seem to celebrate Bob's differences while Doctor Marvin isn't even able to tolerate them. Now it's Marvin's turn to become paranoid. In the climax of the film, Marvin takes Bob out into the woods, determined to dispose of him by using what he calls "death therapy". Things don't turn out the way the doctor expects, and the explosives Marvin uses to dispose of Bob in the end destroy the doctor's home.

DIFFERENCE ISN'T WRONG, IT'S JUST DIFFERENT

What About Bob?

To say *What About Bob?* is my wife's favourite movie would be an understatement; Tina doesn't just *like* this film, she *loves* it. I've lost count how many times she has watched it on her own, or with me, or with a member of the family. Whether it's because of the zany behaviour of the principal character Bob (Bill Murray), the misguided handling of his multi-phobic problems by his psychiatrist (Richard Dreyfuss), the memorable one-liners, or the set pieces highlighting this inappropriate patient-psychiatrist relationship, *What About Bob?* had to be included in the top ten films that sum up my life.

That said, I need to confess that the film is dated now in both form and content. It is very much a film of its times – offensive in its non-PC language and woefully lacking in terms of safeguarding sensitivities. Nonetheless, it does give viewers an insight into the way people handle difficult and at times dysfunctional relationships. The play-off between a neurotic, but loveable New Yorker and a pompous psychiatrist creates a colourful context for exploring some life lessons in interpersonal relationships, lessons that my wife Tina and I have been applying in nearly five decades of marriage.

What About Bob? has created an ongoing dialogue concerning our marriage. For anyone involved in a long-term relationship, a clash of personalities is inevitable. We are different, but different doesn't always mean wrong, it just means different. The attitude of Dr. Marvin towards Bob is faulty; he sees Bob's difference as a problem that needs to be fixed. Dr. Marvin's wife, on the other hand, sees Bob as a person to be accepted, despite these differences. Dr. Marvin cannot celebrate Bob's very different way of thinking and behaving, and it is this that in the end leads to the problem blowing up in his face (quite literally). His wife, meanwhile, sees Bob as someone who needs acceptance, and it is this that in the end leads to Bob being rehabilitated in society. Put succinctly, while Dr. Marvin accepts the problem but fails the person, his family accepts the person and by doing so begins to fix Bob's problem.

This, in many ways, is a picture of how Tina and I respond to people and predicaments. No wonder we have had our heated moments! However, when we have been embroiled in intense discussions, uttering a one-liner from this movie has helped us resolve our differences. Having originally been encouraged to watch this film while studying pastoral theology at Portland Bible College, we have drawn countless relational lessons from its storyline. Since then, *What About Bob?* has become a rite of passage into the Spicer family. All newcomers are exposed to the comedic antics of Bob Wiley (Bill Murray) and the flawed genius of Dr. Leo Marvin (Richard Dreyfuss). Not least, this is designed to help the uninitiated to understand Tina's incessant quotations from the film!

That Tina has embraced 'The Bob Wiley Philosophy' regarding relationships has in some small way enabled her to survive nearly fifty years of being married to one very difficult dude – yes, me! This film, alongside our relationship with God and our biblical beliefs about marriage, has kept us together. It has proved to be a critical factor in resolving conflict.

We're all Different

The truth is, there is an element of Bob Wiley and Dr. Leo Marvin in all of us. We all have zany, different ways of thinking and acting and we also have the tendency to try and fix these things when we see them in others. However, the challenge is to recognise what needs to be *accommodated* and what needs to be either *altered* or *adjusted*. Since relationships are so central to human life, we need to find the best way to engage with those who are different from us and at times difficult to handle. Unless we are going to live in isolation, we must devise a way to embrace rather than exclude difference; not everyone entering our sphere of influence will think, talk and act like us. And thank goodness for that!

While some people fear diversity and prefer to advocate uniformity, the reality is the divine stamp of difference is upon all of us.[108] As such we need to learn to embrace our own differences, as well as those in others. That's what I believe in theory, anyway. However, over the years, my high-sounding theories keep getting mugged by practical living, especially when it comes to married life. Differences aren't always easy to celebrate!

I have come to believe that difference can be part of the divine plan – heaven's way of mirroring God's grace to the world around us.

When he chose his twelve disciples, Jesus took a microcosm of society in order to demonstrate how the Good News can reach everyone, no matter what their cultural, social, fiscal, political or spiritual backgrounds. No two disciples were alike. Matthew was a Jewish tax collector, despised by nationalist countrymen for aiding and abetting the Roman, pagan occupying forces. Simon was a Zealot, part of an insurrectionist movement

---

108. Psalm 139:14.

known for cutting the throats of Roman soldiers and Jewish collaborators. You really can't get more different than that! But Jesus didn't see these two men as problems to be fixed so much as people to accept. Their differences were celebrated, not just tolerated, by him. And in that atmosphere of acceptance, and within the family of the disciples as a group, true transformation began to take place. We shouldn't therefore take the Dr. Marvin approach to the Bobs we meet in life; differences are not always a problem to be fixed. They can be the expression of God-given individuality.

When you think about it, even identical twins have some individual qualities that make them unique. While some see uniformity as a characteristic of a utopian state, the reality is that any environment in which there is no room for difference will not only become bland and boring but will, over time, become abusive and even self-destructive. Difference should, within certain moral, ethical and spiritual boundaries, be welcomed, not criticised. However, only the secure person can fully embrace the difference in others. Only someone who can accept themselves can accept others.

Here we have much to learn from Bob. When describing his failed marriage, Bob Wiley sums up his philosophy of human relationships by saying that there are two types of people in the world, those who love Neil Diamond and those who don't. He then adds laconically that his ex-wife loved him. That's a philosophy different in its own right! Bob totally ignores the fact that he has a multi-phobic personality disorder and that living in constant fear of nearly everything contributed to his marriage break-up. He puts the failure of his marriage down to his wife's musical preference rather than his manic behaviour. Oh, that difference and diversity were simply based on song choice!

Clear and Present Differences

In his bestselling book, *Men are from Mars, Women are from Venus*, John Gray writes, "When men and women are able to respect and accept their difference, then love has a chance to blossom."[109] Whereas I am a classic Type A Personality – competitive, driven, stressed, workaholic – my wife is a Type B Personality – relaxed, patient and friendly. Tina is outgoing, extrovert and social, barely able to stop herself from being involved in a conversation. I, on the other hand, am the shy, self-conscious, reserved, introverted type. In a personality test, Tina would be described as 'enthusiastic, warm, friendly and caring'. I would be described as 'concise, rational, detached and objectively critical'.[110] She loves people and will often need a 'people fix', while I find people draining and easily become 'peopled out'. These are not necessarily the kind of gender-based differences John Gray portrays. They are differences in personality.

Although we have clear and present differences, Tina and I have not allowed these to divide us. We have learnt to use them to our advantage. What I lack, Tina makes up for, and vice versa. Maybe this is one reason why opposites attract and why, more importantly, people with contrasting personalities manage to stay together when they recognise and respect the fact that the insufficiency of one is made up by the sufficiency of the other. A couple can be chalk and cheese in their personality types, but the glue that makes them inseparable is their willingness to *accept* and *respect* their differences. It is also a couple's commonly held *vision* and *values* which enables them to journey together through moments of disagreement.[111] As the Book of Proverbs says, "People without vision fall

---

109. John Gray, *Men Are from Mars, Women Are from Venus*, Harper Collins, p.7.
110. Isabel Briggs Myers, *Introduction to Type*, Oxford Psychologists Press Ltd., 5th Edition.
111. Amos 3:3.

apart."[112] Whether we are lovers of Neil Diamond or not is neither here or there; it is the shared respect and acceptance of difference, as well as a shared vision that forms the adhesive for a long-term attachment.

Some forty years into our marriage I experienced a 'Eureka' moment.

In fairness to Tina, she had been proposing this for years, but while I may have nodded my head in agreement, my mind was not fully open to its acceptance. But on this occasion her words did not fall on deaf ears. I heard what in that moment of time became a revelation: "Difference is not wrong; it's just different." So simple, but so profound! In our interpersonal relationships, we too often over-complicate our journey and end up going around in circles, all because we refuse to pause for a moment, listen hard and find clarity.

In the world of woodworking the dovetail joint is one of the strongest ways of uniting two different pieces of wood. What one-piece of timber lacks, the other possesses; once connected, any pressure the two pieces come under only serves to strengthen the union. In marriage, our unique differences should strengthen our union, not weaken it.

As a married couple with nearly fifty years' experience, I would love to say that Tina and I have never argued or thought of throwing in the towel, but that is not the case. The glue that has kept us together is not some intellectual, emotional or physical bond, but a shared vision of marriage that is deeply spiritual. For us, the covenantal agreement made on 28 December 1971 in a small Mission Hall in Coventry, England,

---

112. Proverbs 29:18, paraphrased.

still holds true today: "For richer, for poorer; in sickness or in health; till death us do part."

As I looked with misty eyes as my beautiful bride approached the altar, my hopes and aspirations were high. If I could go back and talk to that 25-year-old kid, full of testosterone, arrogance and unrealistic expectations, I would tell him to learn faster how to respect and accept difference, to realise that difference in my partner is not wrong, it's just different.

So, then, celebrate the difference in others, and celebrate the difference in you. Be the best you, you can possibly be. Embrace your difference because the divine artist was at work in your creation. Do not allow society's pressures to cause you to shy away from being the unique masterpiece God intended. You were born an original, so don't die a copy. While you may be caught up in a Cinderella culture that manipulates the ugly sisters of intimidation and condemnation to keep you locked in basement thinking rather than high-level living, this is not the life God intended for you. Submitting to this worldly peer pressure will keep you from going to the Ball and celebrating who and what you are in Christ. Allow your differences to be a prism through which the multicoloured grace of God can light up the world around you. God created you with strengths and weaknesses that make you unique, so learn how to draw from the grace of God and become the best version of you that you can possibly be.

Rules of Engagement

How, then, do we celebrate rather than tolerate or subjugate those clear and present differences seen in our *personality* and *perception* of people, objects and events? This is where the film *What About Bob?* comes in to help us. There's a lot we can learn from the characters in this film, not least (ironically) from Bob Wiley (Bill Murray). Sometimes, it's the zany people that have the most to teach us about interpersonal relationships, even if their lessons are more accidental than intended. Dr. Leo Marvin's advice is sound too.

Whereas in our marriage my natural tendency is to lean towards the negative, Tina's positive perception becomes a counterweight that keeps us balanced. In terms of our *personality* type and *perception* tendency, Tina and I are a mixture of Bob Wiley and Dr. Leo Marvin. That Tina *loves* this movie has more to do with its everyday application in handling interpersonal relationships than it does the film's entertainment value. Whereas one personality type might see an obstacle, another sees the opportunity.

A classic illustration of different *perception* is summed up in a famous conversation from the movie *Patch Adams* (1998). Hunter 'Patch' Adams (Robin Williams) is severely depressed and has signed himself into a mental institution. Here he befriends a famous scientist who sets Patch a perception test. Asking him to hold up four fingers, he asks Patch how many fingers he sees, and Patch replies that he sees four. But the scientist wants Patch to look beyond the fingers in a way that creates double vision, resulting in seeing eight fingers. He tells Patch to look beyond the problem, because those who focus on the problem alone fail to see the solution. He then urges him to commit himself to seeing what others choose not to see. If interpersonal relationships have taught me anything, it's the need to look beyond the problem in order to see the solution. In terms of interpersonal relationships, we all need help with our perspective in order to see beyond the problem, in order to find the solution.

1. 'Temporarily Out of Order'

When it comes to our relationships, maybe Bob Wiley's philosophy could prove useful. The Wiley Way is to treat others like telephones. When he meets someone who he thinks doesn't like him, he labels them as temporarily out of order. The task then is not to break the connection – to hang up and then try again.

When it comes to our communication as a couple, and Tina is struggling to get through to me, her angle of approach is to simply tell herself that I am 'temporarily disconnected'. Don't break the connection, maybe try again later. This is a useful tool because it treats emotional disengagement as a temporary problem rather than a permanent condition.

Bob Wiley may be the patient rather than the expert in *What About Bob?* and he may also have suffered the breakdown of his marriage, but he certainly has some good advice about interpersonal communication, including within marriage. This is the heart of our loving Heavenly Father who patiently waits for those who are 'temporarily out of order', never giving up on us when we are choosing to live a life disconnected from him and others.

2. 'Take a Holiday from your Problem'

In a desperate ploy to enjoy his vacation with his family, Dr. Marvin suggests that Bob should take a vacation from his problem. Within the context of the film's story, this is selfish advice. Dr. Marvin just wants to be shot of Bob and his need for constant reassurances. He wants to justify not seeing his patient. But in a general context, it could be deemed good and helpful advice. Sometimes we need to take a break from the pressures of life. So often we become obsessed with our problems. Over-thinking them can leave us in a far worse state. Although there is a fine line between denial and owning our problems, there are times when we need to step away from them for a season.

Leaders need to take a break from people and situations in order recharge their physical, emotional and spiritual batteries.

This is crucial for longevity. Steven R. Covey describes this process as "Sharpening the Saw".[113] As a carpenter, this is something I fully understand. It's frustrating to stop what we are doing in order to restore the cutting edge to the tool we are using. But to work efficiently and effectively, it's essential. This is about "preserving and enhancing the greatest asset you have – YOU".[114] Years of research have concluded that successful, efficient and effective organisations are those that understand the importance of implementing a strategy for self-leadership. So, from your perspective what is the challenge you need to step away from? What does it mean for you to 'sharpen the saw', to 'take a vacation from your problem'?

---

113. Stephen R. Covey, The 7 Habits of Highly Effective People, Simon & Schuster, 1989.
114. Ibid.

How this works in practice will mean different things to different people. For some it will involve turning off their phone or computer, for others in might involve taking a walk, pursuing a hobby, having some shed time, watching a movie or taking some exercise. Whatever it is, the purpose is to do an activity that fixes the mind on something life-enhancing, enjoyable and refreshing, rather than on the problem. That way, when we return to the issue, it doesn't appear so large and can be looked at in a right and balanced perspective.

3. Family Conference

As a highly dysfunctional father figure, Dr. Leo Marvin's way of resolving a domestic crisis is to call for what he describes as a 'family conference'. While this sounds promising in theory, in practice it is not an opportunity for other members of the family to share their opinions and offer some advice. Instead, it's the forum for a control freak to jump to his own conclusions without any thought of arriving at a collective decision.

Learning to listen is a crucial aspect of all interpersonal relationships. Listening does not mean waiting for one person to stop so that you, the overbearing controller, can continue the conversation with what in their mind is a more important part of the dialogue. In case you think I'm judging . . . I've been there and got the T-shirt.

Listening to other people's comments means respecting and accepting their difference – the difference of their personality and perception, that is – as a valid component in reaching an agreed solution. And anyone of us can do this. Even the troubled Bob Wiley becomes a better listener than paid professionals like Dr. Marvin.

And within our marriage, Tina and I have learnt – and are still learning – to have a functional version of Dr. Marvin's 'family conference', ones in which both or all parties get to have a say, where everyone's differences are accepted and respected, and where everyone's voice is heard. From the bedroom to the boardroom, this is sound advice.

4. Beating Yourself Up

One of the great comedic set pieces in the film occurs after a night-long storm in which Bob has had to stay over at Dr. Marvin's house. This puts the doctor on edge, which is unfortunate because that next morning he is due to be filmed at home about his new book, *Baby Steps*. When the interviewer arrives, she meets Bob, who is introduced as one of Marvin's patients, and she insists that the patient is included in the interview. Dr. Marvin is livid and puts in a poor performance during the live sequence. Bob, on the other hand, shines! He answers all the interviewer's questions about *Baby Steps*, telling stories that indicate that the book has been a gamechanger in his recovery. In the end, the psychiatrist fails dismally to commend his own book, while the patient paints the book, and its theories, in glowing colours.

Following his disastrous television appearance with *Good Morning America* to promote his latest book *Baby Steps*, Dr. Marvin is inconsolable. Having practiced his poise, prepared his speech and decided on his preferred fireplace shot, the event has been gatecrashed by Bob Wiley who, when Dr. Leo freezes, steals the show. For the doctor, this is a train wreck, hence his pathetic cry to his wife that it had been a disaster.

When, on Easter Sunday Evening 1968, Tina first attended my home church, I was unfortunately away preaching and had to wait till the following day to catch sight of this gorgeous, effervescent, outgoing young lady. In the half a century since then, she has always been my 'Faye' – someone who has helped me maintain a true perspective on my numerous preaching/teaching events.

For me, the aftermath of public speaking is not always pretty.

It may come as a surprise to non-public-speakers reading this, but preachers are known to have moments of deep discouragement in the wake of their talks. As one who internalises things, I tend to be forensic with my post-mortem; mentally dissecting my words, inflections, pace, preparation and delivery, I leave no stone unturned in the search for excellence. In terms of congregational response, I rerun the tape in my mind to remember whether I could see what conductor Ben Zander called 'shining eyes'. Preachers are a rare breed, regularly suffering from post-preaching blues. Over a half a century of preaching I have often found my Dr. Marvin personality saying, *"It was disastrous, Tina!"* to which she will bring a different and much needed perspective to my negativity.

To me preaching is a privilege. That people in this highly visual world would give their time to sit and listen to a speaker is something I do not take for granted. Whether to an audience of 12 or 1,200, the preparatory effort is the same. For every minute of presentation there are hours of preparation. But then having emptied one's self of what has taken days to prepare, a physical, emotional and spiritual vacuum is created that makes a speaker vulnerable to either negative or positive thoughts, actions or reactions. To restore the soul, resting the body and reviving the spirit through reading, relaxing, exercising, listening to or talking with supportive people, is crucial.

We all need the Fayes of this world, those who lovingly bring balance to the extremes in our responses.

Take Baby Steps

Human relationships are complex, and it takes time to develop the strategies I've mentioned above – time and a lot of commitment, energy and hard work. Accepting and respecting the differences in other people within your sphere of influence does not happen in a moment. It happens over time. Similarly, it takes a lot of wisdom and discernment to know what things in other people's lives need to be accommodated and what need to be altered. Marriage is a lifelong journey of mutual transformation. This transformation is not a matter of one person controlling and manipulating another person to conform to their expectations. That, to use another movie title, is the stuff of *Gaslight*. No, as the song goes, 'love changes everything'. Over a lifetime, love changes wounded hearts into healed hearts, unhappy pasts into hopeful futures. This is the power of love. It accepts the differences that are part of our uniqueness and alters those differences that are symptomatic of our woundedness.

Like so much of the doctor's advice in the movie, the central premise of his book is sensible and healthy. The idea he explores is this: that it is more productive to set small attainable goals than to struggle to make huge quantum strides. When the doctor first tells Bob about his thesis, Bob enthusiastically begins 'baby-stepping' out of the office, down the corridor and into the elevator. The screams coming from the elevator tell the viewer that progress will be gradual. In the end, Bob's recovery will not be through the doctor's counselling but through being accepted by the doctor's family, one step at a time.

In terms of improving our relationships, change is gradual. We might prefer to take 'one giant leap', but lasting change comes through taking small steps, *baby* steps. Perhaps this is what the prophet Isaiah had in mind when he encouraged us to embrace biblical truth "line upon line, here a little, there a little".[115] Interpersonal relationships are incredibly challenging. However, deep and long-lasting fulfilment can happen through taking small incremental steps.

When someone is having a hard time engaging emotionally, a baby step involves seeing that person as temporarily disconnected, not permanently detached.

When someone is over-thinking a problem, a baby step means taking a holiday from the issue, even if that's just for a few hours.

When someone is feeling disempowered or frustrated, a baby step might mean holding a family conference in which their true feelings are heard.

Baby-stepping our way to a better marriage, partnership or relationship is a slow process and we rush it at our peril. Taking minute steps toward a common goal is the answer. As the old Chinese Proverb says, "A journey of a thousand miles begins with one single step." Although we will undoubtedly experience setbacks, as "partakers of the divine nature",[116] we will by God's grace achieve our long-term goal by taking small incremental steps.

As you can see, there's a lot of wisdom in *What About Bob?*

KEEPING IT REEL

Mistakes I Have Made:
- Saying the wrong thing at the wrong time.
- Not accepting and respecting difference.
- Using coercion.
- Being more task than relationship orientated.

---

115. Isaiah 28:10, ESV.
116. 2 Peter 1:4.

Lessons I Have Learnt:

- Difference isn't wrong; it's just different.
- To take a vacation from my problem.
- Listen more, talk less.
- Be the best 'you' possible.

CHAPTER

Dedicated to the memory of
Chris Sutton
1974–1999
'Honour Him'

TRAILER

Gladiator (2000) is a Roman epic movie directed by Sir Ridley Scott and starring Russell Crowe as Maximus, the General who becomes a slave. After the Emperor Marcus Aurelius decides that his own son Commodus (Joachim Phoenix) doesn't have what it takes to carry out his wishes after his death, he chooses Maximus instead. Commodus, learning this, kills his father and then orders the execution of Maximus. Maximus escapes but learns that Commodus has murdered his wife and son and robbed him of his lands and home. His life ruined, Maximus is captured by slave traders and sold to become a gladiator in North Africa. He becomes a famous and unbeatable fighter, an accolade which ultimately leads him to return to Rome, where he confronts his nemesis – Commodus, now a self-indulgent and amoral Emperor – in the Colosseum. A final battle ensues in which the gladiator is revealed to be the General, much loved and honoured by the inhabitants of the Roman Empire. When Commodus kills him, Maximus has a vision of being reunited with his wife and son in the fields of Elysium. Thus, he dies by the same beliefs with which he has lived, that everything we do in this life echoes in eternity. *Gladiator* is a film with many Christian undertones. Like Jesus, who became a slave so that we who are slaves might become free, Maximus is the General who becomes a slave, so that those enslaved to an evil Emperor might have their liberty!

HONOUR HIM

Gladiator

The psychological impact and social influence a movie can have on an audience is immense. Both Hitler and Stalin knew this; they successfully used films throughout World War II for propaganda purposes. While the primary purpose of a movie is to make profit through entertainment – cinemagoers must find the experience engaging and engrossing, after all – some producers see entertainment as secondary purpose behind the greater goal of changing opinions and outlooks on life. Playing with viewer's minds, producers have long understood the power of cinema to influence thoughts and feelings.

While there have been, and still are, film producers and directors who want to exploit the visual power of film for propagandist purposes, most are content to evoke simple emotional responses in audiences. They know that anger, joy, fear, shock and sadness can all be triggered by a movie moment. In a matter of seconds, the viewer can be transported from the depths of despair to the heights of ecstasy. Some viewers, of course, resist the emotive appeal of films. The same film-lover that blames their watery eyes on seasonal allergies can easily suppress their fears or subdue their laughter. When watching a scary home movie full of suspense, Tina will need her trusty cushion to silence her screams, and I usually excuse myself from watching the tensest scenes. These reactions are not untypical; they are signs of how successful films can be in evoking some of our deepest, even primal, emotions.

While some movies mess with our brains, others remind us of things we would much rather forget.

Great movies inspire us to dream big and pursue a life of passion. They show us how to overcome life's obstacles, how not to let our circumstances define us, and how to maintain a positive attitude in the face of a perceived enemy. Great films not only challenge us to conquer our fears and live our present in the light of an ultimate, they encourage us to stand up for what is right and battle all opposing factors to the point of victory. This is at least in part the reason why *Gladiator* is the penultimate film in *The Reel Story*.

Be warned, however: *Gladiator* is R rated for good reasons. It is bloody, extremely violent and not for the fainthearted, containing occasional coarse language. Despite these things, I have lost count how many times I have watched this movie. I love the action scenes and the original musical score, composed by Hans Zimmer. The brilliant acting by the principal players is both engaging and memorable. This is truly a great movie.

Released in 2000, *Gladiator* made its grand entrance at the dawn of the new millennium, grossing $457 million in world sales. The position for number one millennial movie was a closely fought contest between *Gladiator* and *Crouching Tiger, Hidden Dragon*. Winning five Oscars – Best Actor, Best Picture, Best Costume Design, Best Sound and Best Visual Effect – *Gladiator* became the must-watch movie of the year. But it's not these human accolades that have earned *Gladiator* a place in my top ten. Rather, it's the fact that it forms the perfect backdrop to speaking of the life and legacy of one extraordinary individual, someone who lived his life with a sense of urgency and passion, a young man who fought an epic battle before entering the afterlife, someone whose brief time amongst us still resonates with those who knew him.

No Place like Rome

Gladiator is set in AD 180, at a time when Roman rule throughout the known world, while vast and extensive, was beginning to wane. The movie transports the audience on a partial tour of the Roman Empire, opening in Germania with one of the most brutal and vivid battle scenes in cinematic history – today Germania would cover a major part of Europe – before travelling with slave traders from Spain to Northern Africa, and then eventually taking us back to a troubled Rome. There, in the capital city, a kind of cold war takes place between the Emperor and the Senate as the sun begins slowly to set on the Roman Empire. The imperial dream had been cast in almost biblical language: "Rome is the light" while the rest of the world "is brutal and cruel and dark". Now it seems the light of the Roman Empire itself is beginning to dim, and its people increasingly doomed to enter a dark age themselves.

Maximus Decimus Meridius (Russell Crowe) is a powerful and much-loved general of the Roman legions in Europe. His arch enemy is the son of the Emperor Marcus Aurelius who planned to return the rule of the Roman Empire to the Senate and the people. Marcus Aurelius' intention was to have his favourite General, Maximus Decimus Meridius, oversee the transition. This enraged the Emperor's son Commodus (Joachim Phoenix). Having been side-lined in favour of the general, Commodus kills his father and arranges the execution of Maximus, along with the murder of Maximus' wife and child. However, Maximus escapes his executioners and flees to Spain. Here he finds his property destroyed and his wife and son burnt alive and crucified. Mourning his loss, the one-time powerful solider of Rome is taken by slave traders to be trained as a gladiator in Northern Africa. When eventually he finds himself fighting as a gladiator back in Rome's Colosseum, Maximus takes the advice of the wealthy slave trader, Proximo (Oliver Reed), to be the best he needs to win the crowd. This he does and once again he becomes an irritant in the evil-hearted Commodus. As a threat to forces of darkness gathering over the Roman Empire, Commodus plots the former General's death. This occurs in a memorable and dramatic final battle between the upstart Emperor Commodus and the slave who once fought for Rome as its finest General.

The closing words of the movie speak of a good man, a soldier of Rome, to whom those looking on were told, "Honour him." These words not only conclude the movie, they set the scene for this chapter.

Honour Him

"Why," you might ask, "use such a bloodthirsty film to speak of the life of someone near and dear?" The answer is simple: To honour the memory of a spiritual solider, a servant of the king of all kings who fought an epic battle and won. The inclusion of *Gladiator* in my top ten films for *The Reel Story* gives me the opportunity to highlight the remarkable life of a much-loved and sadly missed young man.

A life, though tragically short, that teaches us not only how to live but how to die.

In this chapter, we will come face-to-face with the brevity of life and our own mortality. Here we face the reality of faith and doubt, the unanswered questions that sorrow brings and some pointers concerning finding hope in the midst of tragedy.

Gladiator as a movie is one epic battle from beginning to end, a fight that earns one man the honour he justly deserves.

What 1992 was for her majesty Queen Elizabeth II, 1999 was for my family. Not that we suffered any family fallout, far from it; this year, in fact, created even stronger bonds. Neither did we experience the tragedy of our family home catching fire. Nevertheless 1999 was, to use the words of Queen Elizabeth II, an *annus horribilis* – a horrible year.

Having returned from Portland Bible College with a theology degree, our second daughter Hannah had become friendly with a young man by the name of Christopher Sutton – Chris to family and friends. Chris was a University and Bible College graduate with a strong Christian faith. A friendship between Hannah and Chris soon began to thrive. When they began to enjoy and express a sense of destiny for their lives together, Tina and I saw Chris as a welcome addition to our family and Hannah and Chris as possibly ideal candidates for future leadership in a fledgling church we were attempting to establish.

With the backing of the church leadership, our plan was to pioneer a church in the nation's second city, Birmingham. Tina and I tried our best to hold down full-time jobs while pioneering a new congregation. This grew from a community occupying an art gallery basement to one using the Birmingham Repertory Theatre. The task of leadership was made somewhat easier by recognising the emerging leadership we saw in Hannah and Chris.

Chris was a great guy, kind, generous and thoughtful. He was people-friendly and a servant-hearted leader who could communicate biblical truth in a relevant way. Welcoming him into our family with open arms, we found that his zeal, passion, sense of humour and passion for spiritual things was contagious. Here was a young man who was spiritually natural and naturally spiritual. Following in the footsteps of his pastoring parents, Chris was a lover and encourager of people. Having grown up with the values we sought to sow into our children, Chris soon became a vital part of our household and a wonderful future son-in-law.

Engaged to Hannah, Chris had not only found the girl of his dreams but together they had managed to secure a mortgage on a lovely cottage. After living in student digs for many years, Chris craved a home of his own. With their marriage plans well in hand, the church was booked, as was the wedding reception venue. Life was good and the future looked full of shared and exciting possibilities.

Little did we know that Chris was not well! Having repeatedly complained of tiredness and back pains, the doctors thought it might be a viral, muscular, or urinary inflection. One even suggested that Chris might be suffering from depression. Eventually, the doctor sent him for an X-ray. This being inconclusive, they requested more and more tests. As Easter approached, our concerns began to grow.

Good Friday 1999 was not a good day.

As many took the opportunity to meet with family and friends, Tina and I were requested to join Chris, Hannah and his parents for a meeting with a consultant. As we entered the office of the oncology consultant in Queen Elizabeth Hospital, Birmingham, we could tell by the look on everyone's faces the news was bad. By the time we arrived, the hospital staff had left the room, leaving the family to come to terms with the dreadful news.

Words like 'Cancer', 'Inoperable', 'Incurable', 'Terminal' hung in the air like storm clouds. Chris was slumped against a table with Hannah's arm around him, something both she and Sue,

Chris's mum, would be called to do more and more in the coming weeks. His face was ashen, while shock and horror were mirrored in the faces of everyone in the room.

Chris had a type of cancer normally found in old people that would typically be slow in its development, but when found in younger people was rapid. Kidney cancer had spread to his lungs. Chris faced this with great bravery and tranquillity. As the consultant would later write in a letter, "He was an amazing young man and his calm and courage impressed us all. It was very harrowing for all of us who played a part in looking after him particularly as we had so little to offer."[117] Chris would undergo surgery to remove his cancerous kidney, but this was done merely to lessen the pain.

Strength and Honour

Gladiator salutes the memory of a brave individual who fought an epic battle. It has become to me a spiritual milestone, a marker in the journey of life. As I watch the final battle that Maximus fought against Commodus and won, I am reminded of Chris's mammoth conflict with cancer. He too was about to enter the arena for a final time and would exit carried on the shoulders of those who loved and knew him.

Chris was 25 years old – the same age I was when I married Tina. He had his whole life in front of him and everything to live for – a bride-to-be, a beautiful home, a new job and a promising career. But nothing, absolutely nothing could prepare him or us for this devastating news or what lay ahead.

Standing in that consultant's room surrounded by shell-shocked people, all I can remember is Chris's father saying, "This isn't real. It feels as if I am in an episode of *Casualty*." But, sadly, this was no television drama. This was real life.

---

117. Mr D. M. A. Wallace, University Hospital Birmingham, letter dated 16 June 1999.

Here was a man whose life lay shattered like pieces of a priceless antique vase on the floor. What could I possibly say that might begin to pick up the pieces? A deadly disease was conspiring to cut his life short. Right now, he needed to hear words of faith to silence the fears, truth to dispel the doubt and comfort to calm the storm. With all the faith I could muster I said, "Well Chris it may be true what the doctors say, but the truth is, God can heal you!" Deep inside I would have preferred to say nothing. I simply wanted to run, shout, scream, "No, this can't be true. God, why?" Right then a cacophony of shouts and thoughts where filling my head. I was sad, angry, fearful, desperate for someone to tell us they had got it all wrong.

Although Chris kindly acknowledged my words, I have no idea how he was holding it together. Hannah was then, as she would be over the coming weeks, right by his side, caring for him with a love and concern that made me so proud. In the later weeks of Chris's life, both Hannah and Sue, Chris's mum, would undertake a 24/7 vigil at his bedside. Hannah would place her life on hold to become God's gift to Chris.

While appreciating the reality of the doctor's diagnosis and the medical help the hospital gave them, Chris and Hannah had an unshakeable faith that God would heal him. Even when a consultant tried to prepare Hannah for the inevitable by using words like 'choking' and 'suffocating' to describe the manner of his death, she politely thanked him and quickly returned to Chris's bedside. As Hannah's father, I found myself in unfamiliar territory. How do you approach the possibility that Chris might not be healed without crushing their faith? How do I suggest to Chris that he write a letter to Hannah only to be opened in the event of his death? Sadly, rightly or wrongly, I did neither.

Over the coming weeks, Chris would spend time at our home, in hospital and then within hours of his passing in a hospice. It was eight weeks from diagnosis to death. Over that time, it was if we were sat in some ancient Roman amphitheatre watching a gladiatorial battle taking place. The fight Chris was involved in, like the final battle of Maximus, seemed unfairly balanced. Matching blow for blow, Chris seemed to take it all in his stride. While the oxygen helped his breathing, the morphine kept his pain in check, and yet his deterioration was visible for all to see. In saluting these two victors, *strength* goes to Hannah, as *honour* goes to Chris. Their unwavering faith and their unfailing love were like crocuses in the desert.

I have conducted numerous funerals, but nothing like this.

The small church was full to overflowing with people listening outside. Reuben Morgan's song, 'This Is My Desire', beautifully described a life dedicated to the service of God in a service we called 'A Celebration'. We all tried our best to celebrate, but beneath strong exteriors, people were crumbling under the weight of grief.

Trying my best to offer words of encouragement, I spoke of the 'Cul-de-sac of Confusion', the 'Avenue of Anguish' and the 'Lanes of Loneliness' we were all travelling.

While I sought to offer comfort to family and friends, the reality was Chris was gone.

The closing comments were taken from the diary of another 25-old college graduate who, a few years before being martyred in the Ecuadorian Jungle as a Christian missionary, wrote,

'He makes his ministers a flame of fire.'
Am I ignitable?
God deliver me from the dread asbestos of 'other things'.

Saturate me with the oil of the Spirit that I may be aflame.
But a flame is transient, often short-lived.
Canst thou bear this, my soul – short life?
In me there dwells the Spirit of the Great short-lived, whose
zeal for God's house consumed Him. Make me thy fuel, flame
of God.[118]

So, with the theme tune of *Honour Him* playing in my mind, this chapter is written to honour the memory of a young man who not only taught us how to live but also, in the words of my wife Tina, "He showed us how to die!"

My name is Maximus ...

In one of the most memorable scenes from *Gladiator*, a soldier who through no fault of his own had become a slave makes a statement that still resonates today.

Although becoming a gladiator was normally a death sentence, Maximus had garrisoned his fellow slaves to fight against the odds and win a momentous battle in the Roman amphitheatre. At the very end, Commodus commands this former general to remove his helmet and identify himself. Having initially responded by telling them that he is Gladiator, in an act of defiance he turns his back on the Emperor. This further enrages Commodus.

The Gladiator's fellow slaves are now surrounded by the feared Praetorian Guard and they are readying themselves to die. Turning to face Commodus, who has no idea as to the Spaniard's true identity, the Gladiator removes his metal mask. In one of those inspiring, hair-raising, goose bump moments, the man begins to speak. He tells them his name – Maximus Decimus Meridius. He tells them his rank – Commander of

---

118. Elisabeth Elliot, *Through Gates of Splendour*, STL, 1980.

the armies of the North and General of the Felix Legions. He tells them of his allegiance – loyal servant to the true Emperor of Rome, Marcus Aurelius. He tells them of his family – he's a father to a murdered son and a husband to a murdered wife. And finally, he tells them of his mission – to have vengeance either in this life or in the life to come.

What an extraordinary, heroic statement of identity!

Chris Sutton knew his identity too. Refusing to be defined by the disease that was attacking his body, like so many before and since he would dare to say, "I may have cancer, but cancer does not have me!" Like Maximus, Chris was a leader, a servant-solider, not of Rome but of the one true God. He was a spiritual father to many, a partner of a much-loved future wife, a spiritual father to numerous spiritual children, someone who sought the redemption of many and lived his life with eternity in mind.

Like Maximus, Chris lived his life with passion, and he earned the applause of those around him.

A born leader, Chris was brave in the face of the enemy, someone who lived his life with an awareness of eternity. He therefore lived with a sense of urgency; he fought and won an amazing battle, believing that "what you do in this life echoes in eternity".

When Chris's earthly flame was extinguished on the morning of 28 May 1999, a darkness descended over me that left me stumbling around in a fog of unanswered questions. One word ran through my befuddled mind – why? While I tried to see God's bigger picture and His sovereignty, I also tried to believe "that in all these things we are more than conquerors through him who loved us. For we are sure that neither death nor life, nor angels, nor rules, nor things present nor things to come, nor powers, nor height nor depth, nor anything else in all creation, will be able to separate us from the love of God in Christ Jesus our Lord."[119]

While Tina drew comfort from a loving Heavenly Father, Hannah entered a season of believing God but being unable to trust him.

I, meanwhile, grew more and more desperate for answers.

Once, when discussing suffering with my university professor, I had encouraged him to read Philip Yancey's book, *Where Is God When It Hurts?* Without shying away from the problem of pain, Yancey concludes by answering his own question, "Where is God when it hurts? He transforms pain, using it to teach and strengthen us, if we allow it to turn us toward him."[120]

Yancey concluded that God is where he has always been, by our side, for "He will never leave us or forsake us."[121]

No wonder my professor acknowledged this to be the best book he had ever read on suffering.

Unprepared for Tragedy

The agony of watching your child go through the loss of a loved one and the grief that follows are things no parent wants to experience. At times, Hannah's grief seemed unbearable and at other times she wondered if life was worth living. It could only have been the grace of God that kept her pursuing a purpose in life. Today she is once again able to trust God, to believe in his sovereignty, and can see the redemptive arc in that season of her life.

---

119. Romans 8:38–39.
120. Philip Yancey, *Where Is God When It Hurts?* Marshall Pickering, 1977, p.256.
121. Hebrews 13:5.

Fathers are by nature fixers!

Standing around Chris's hospice bed just minutes after his passing, Hannah didn't need to say anything. I knew what she wanted me to do. Pre-empting her request, I asked if she wanted me to pray for Chris to be raised from the dead. Her positive response did little to raise my level of expectation.

At that moment, I felt spiritually inept. Battling failure as a father, I wanted so much to fix things. My daughter wanted her beloved back and neither I, nor my prayer, could do a thing about it. In general, Christians do not do well with death and disease, lacking any practical theology regarding our own mortality. Knowing theoretically that death comes to us all, we will try everything to avoid the inevitable. That was true of us too.

Having allowed my family to experience an excessive emphasis on faith and positivity, we were unprepared for tragedy. The Christian organisation we had spent twelve years in overtly and covertly encouraged everyone to put on a brave face, to project an image that said everything was good, even if it wasn't. Caught up in this somewhat hyper-faith and highly positive movement, people became discouraged and disenfranchised because they had imbibed a theology of healing and non-healing that was woefully lacking in spiritual honesty. Shying away from our own mortality, death and disease became a taboo subject that few wanted to discuss. Burying our head in the sand only left us exposed in other areas. Although I would prefer to exit this life in the manner my mother did – having what I believe was an angelic visitation, she simply fell to the ground and passed from this life to the next in moment of time – none of us can dictate the time or way of our death.

However, there are some things I learnt through this experience and I'd like to pass these on to you about what not to do. As the saying goes, never waste a good trial.

- **Killing them with Kindness** – For a father, hindsight may inspire honesty that may or may not be helpful. Looking back at Chris's passing, I would have to say that I did a poor job in preparing my children for tragedy. Yes, the church environment in which they spent most of their formative years did preach an unhelpful gospel of positivity and prosperity, but rather than blame shift, I need to take responsibility.

Knowing that there is no such person as a perfect parent, I raise my hand to confess the fact that I did little to introduce my children to life's negativity and poverty. Looking back, I wish that I had taken each of my children on a visit to a Third World country to see life from a less Western, consumeristic and comfortable perspective. Do not get me wrong, Tina and I have raised four wonderful children. Esther, Luther, Hannah and Jonathan are my north, south, east and west on life's compass. But exposing them to both the haves and have-nots might have created in each of them a more realistic view of the brevity of life.

- **Questioning the Almighty** – In Chris's death, Tina and I faced his departure very differently. While I wanted answers, Tina acknowledged the sovereignty of God in all situations. Refusing to believe this his life was taken through evil activity, she remained a tower of strength, secure in her belief in the sovereignty of a loving Heavenly Father. I, meanwhile, was full of questions. While divine healing is a majestic work of God, either with or without medical care, answered or unanswered prayer in terms of healing is still a mystery.

It's important to remember that the God we serve is not angered by or annoyed with our tantrums in the times of tragedy. He is big enough and loving enough to listen to our shouts of "Why?" Our accusations of wrongdoing do not faze him but cause him to draw closer and "quieten us with his love".[122]

- **Blame shifting** – "Who sinned, this man or his parents?"[123] Human beings long to find someone responsible for their difficulties. Since Adam blamed Eve for their predicament, humans have tried to find comfort and consolation by dumping the blame on someone else. I did the same, blaming doctors, diet, delay and poor decisions. But I found nothing or no one to ease the pain. The difficulty of trying to pastor a family and church through a season of mourning only added to the sense of being adrift in an ocean of uncertainty. Having released the blame from your clenched fist, you hope that by being empty-handed you might find an antidote to your empty heart. You don't.

- **Dealing with Doubt** – Doubt is a door that takes you into the room of human reasoning. Here logic, understanding, perception and knowledge argue the case at hand. While disappointment might bring you here, doubt is a place we reside in at our peril.

Coming from a root word that means 'two', doubt puts you in two minds. While the English phrase 'having a foot in both camps' might adequately describe this double-mindedness, I much prefer the Chinese version of 'having a foot in two boats'.

For a while, a healthy understanding of doubt is okay. However, sooner or later we will have to decide which boat we are going to enter.

---

122. Zephaniah 3:17, paraphrased.
123. John 9:1–7, ESV.

What we do now reverberates into our eternal future.

This is for me the finest thought from the movie *Gladiator*. Both Maximus and Christopher Sutton lived by the sentiments of this saying. To take the title of another great movie, both men knew what it meant to *Pay it Forward* into eternity. Both men lived their immediate in the light of an ultimate, refusing to let their circumstances define them, living every day with a passion for the present as well as for the future.

Although rarely talked about in this fast moving, here-and-now society, Christianity is a faith that focuses on the afterlife. This life is a drop in the ocean and one day this space-time continuum will be wrapped up to make room for eternity. To live our immediate in the light of an ultimate helps us, like Chris, to live life with a sense of urgency. From my vantage point, I can look back and say with absolute certainty, life is short. This is the written legacy my mother left me, penned in the margins of a biblical text. No matter how old we are, in the light of eternity we all have little time. We should remember the saying, "Life is short and full of uncertainties, so live each day as if was your last."

Although humanly speaking, Chris Sutton's brief existence is characterised by a dash – the one between 1974 and 1999 – how he lived between his birth and death is what truly defines his life. And what better way to conclude this chapter than by using the closing words of the film, when following the death of Maximus, his closet alia Juba said, "We will see you again, but not yet!"

Chris Sutton, it is my heartfelt belief that "We will see you again, but not yet!"

KEEPING IT REEL

Mistakes I Have Made:
- Not helping my children to handle tragedy.
- Staying too long in the room of uncertainty.
- Failing to live my immediate in the light of the ultimate.
- Allowing circumstances to define me.

Lessons I Have Learnt:
- What we do in life echoes in eternity.
- Everyone needs a passion to live for.
- Life is short and full of uncertainties so live each day as if it's your last.
- Where is God when it hurts? He is right beside you.

CHAPTER

TRAILER

Mr. Holland's Opus (1995) is a stirring and moving film about a music teacher called Glenn Holland (Richard Dreyfuss) in Portland, Oregon. Having always wanted to be a composer, and having missed out on the opportunity, Holland is compelled to find work and income as a high-school music teacher. However, his love of classical music alienates him from his pupils who are much more interested in Rock & Roll. At the same time, things at home are challenging; Holland's son is deaf and his marriage is suffering because of his frustration at not fulfilling his dream of performing his magnum opus that will hopefully bring him fame and fortune. In the end, Holland decides to use Rock & Roll to connect with his class and from then on grows closer to his students but further from his son. He continues to inspire his students for many years, while giving less and less time to his family and to his orchestral masterpiece. Until, one day, it's too late. There's no more time to have his *opus* funded or performed. Budget cuts lead to music being eliminated from the school curriculum and Holland must take early retirement. The chance to perform his life's work has seemingly gone. He feels that his legacy is lost and that he's a failure. But there's a surprise in store for Mr. Holland. And to enjoy it, you'll need to see the movie for yourself. Make sure you have plenty of tissues. And make sure you give careful thought to what legacy you're leaving as well!

LIFE IN THE LAST LANE

Mr. Holland's Opus

When we grew old and move from the middle lane to the last lane, we automatically check the rear-view mirror to see what lies behind us. In the case of a car driver, this action is momentary, a mere glance rather than a prolonged gaze. In the case of a person of mature years, it can mean a sustained and wistful preoccupation.

Living life in the rear-view mirror is potentially disastrous, not just in cars but in life. The biblical Jesus put it like this, *"No one who puts his hand to the plough and looks back is fit for the kingdom of God."*[124] To look back in order to take pride in our achievements not only takes our eyes off our God-given goal, it can also result in us failing to forge a straight furrow in which others can follow. Later in Luke's gospel Jesus refers to Lot's wife who, although being told not to, looked back towards the immoral cities of Sodom and Gomorrah and was turned into a pillar of salt.[125] Jesus was reminding his listeners that kingdom living is life on God's terms, not ours. As in the natural so in the spiritual, the exercise of looking back should only be entertained as part of the process of moving forward.

And this brings me to the last film in *The Reel Story* – a film, like the one in my first chapter, focuses on a teacher determined to leave a legacy.

I'm talking about *Mr. Holland's Opus*.

It's not simply because this movie was filmed on location during the year we lived in Portland, Oregon, nor is it simply

---

124. Luke 9:62, ESV. Emphasis added.
125. Luke 17:32; Genesis 19:26.

because we had the opportunity to be extras in the crowd scenes! It's because the storyline creates the kind of glorious crescendo to life I would dearly love to experience.

Glenn Holland (Richard Dreyfuss) wonders if his life has reached its full potential. As a musical performer, he had wanted to compose a musical opus that would have given him fame and fortune. That dream is now fast becoming a distant memory. Having to adopt a fall-back position as a high school music teacher, checking his rear-view mirror now reminds him that this is not the life he had intended. Dead dreams, dashed hopes and abandoned aspirations have made the last thirty years for Mr. Holland a painful reminder of the twists and turns his life has unexpectedly taken. Having made the transition from the middle lane to last lane, I find myself empathising with the closing frames of *Mr. Holland's Opus* – wondering whether my life will be a *legacy* for others enjoy, or a *liability* for them to endure.

At the age of sixty, Glenn Holland has little hope of ever working again. Now it's his last day of employment and the beginning of his retirement. With three decades of classroom paraphernalia bundled into a cardboard box, he, along with his wife and his son Cole, makes his way to the school exit. Thrown onto the educational scrapheap and surplus to requirements, Mr. Holland is reluctantly manoeuvring himself into the last lane. It's strange to think that the teaching career he entered kicking and screaming he is now so reluctant to leave.

The Hollywood producers now treat the viewing public to one of the best grand finales of 20th-century cinema entertainment.

On exiting the school for one final time, Holland hears some non-timetabled music coming from the auditorium. Its music that does not resonate with how he is feeling. His inner song is more of a lament played in a minor key.

Mr. Holland is about to face the music big time.

He is about to be confronted with his legacy.

Life in the Last Lane

Through ten movies, *The Reel Story* is an attempt to tell my story, to share the mistakes made and lessons learnt from a lifetime involved in different streams of Christianity, business and social enterprise. All of this is written with the sole intention of helping others avoid the mistakes I have made and to inspire the next generation to break through the glass ceiling my generation may have inadvertently created.

In short, this book is about my legacy.

That anyone from my generation would leave this life without sharing his or her knowledge, wisdom and experience to an emerging generation would, in my opinion, be an irretrievable tragedy.

What if Dr Martin Luther King Jr. had never shared his dream?

What if Einstein had kept his theories to himself or Leonardo da Vinci never sketched his vision of the future?

I am determined not to let this happen, which is why in this book there had to be an element of sharing my story. I have simply had to talk of those people, objects and events that have either helped or hindered me in a journey lasting what in biblical terms is "three score years and ten".[126] Hopefully, *The Reel Story* will encourage others to discover a purpose bigger than themselves and pursue it with a burning passion. No matter how your education, experience or environment conspires to hold you back, with God's grace I believe that you can break free of the negative and pursue the positive.

In all of this, I am learning to see life in the last lane as a positive not a negative reality, as an opportunity not an obstacle. Age is an attitude, an angle of approach to life based on our *beliefs* that in turn affects our *behaviour* and ultimately what we *become*. I have met old people in their thirties, and I've met young people in their sixties.

---

126. Psalm 90:10, KJV.

Age is not just a number; it's a mindset, a way of thinking for which we must all take responsibility.

My human body may be finite and wearing, but by God's grace I can seek to renew my mind daily.

From our mid-twenties, certain changes take place in our body. Our bones lose calcium and become more brittle. Our skin loses its elasticity. Age spots begin to appear and when we look at our hands, we see our parents' hands. We are losing brains cells at a phenomenal rate. All the while, our weight begins to shift south and our hair stops growing where we want it to and begins to grow in places no hair has grown on us before.

If you're young and saying to yourself, "That will never happen to me! I will never grow old like that!" Along with my fellow senior citizens, I would like to say, "We understand, and we love you, but it will happen to you and frankly we are looking forward to it."[127]

Old age creeps up on us all. Sooner or later – sooner than you realise – you too will be gazing into your rear-view mirror, wondering what your life was all about, hoping that you've left something of significance in the world you're closer to leaving than entering.

Like Mr. Holland, I find myself gathering my thoughts as I walk towards the exit of five decades of working life wondering what my legacy will be. Without becoming morbid or nostalgic, I want to leave a straight furrow in which others can follow. I do not want to look back and become trapped in some time warp. Preserving those godly elements of the past, I want to prepare for the future, whatever that involves.

---

127. This paragraph is indebted to a sermon entitled 'The King has the Last Move' by John Ortberg, Willow Creek Organization.

As the Apostle Paul said when considering life in the last lane, "I press on toward the goal for the prize of the upward call of God in Christ Jesus."[128]

Science of the Swing

As adults, we may regret a misspent youth. As parents, we may feel remorse for wasted years. As spouses, we may want to revisit squandered opportunities. As employees, we may want the opportunity to redress those idle years. As investors, we may long to renege on those bad deals. All this is human and understandable.

But life in the rear-view mirror is only helpful if it prepares us to move forward.

In mechanical terms, this is known as the 'Science of the Swing'. Whether it's a golf swing, tennis shot or a child's garden swing, science tells us that our backward movement equals forward momentum. No sportsperson would dare to ignore the importance of the backward swing in relation to their forward projection. The same is true for looking back on our lives. Rather than letting regret and remorse freeze us in time, we should live in a redemptive way by allowing our past to push us forward into all that lies ahead.

With retirement looming, Glenn Holland finds himself in unfamiliar territory. This is a critical moment for which he is totally unprepared, one that could send him on a downward spiral. Becoming a music teacher was his fall-back solution. It wasn't his dream.

---

128. Philippians 3:14, ESV.

In this scenario, I can empathise with Glenn Holland. Having been called to preach, I have over the last fifty years found it necessary to take on work outside of the church setting. Having taken my father's advice to complete a five-year apprenticeship as a carpenter and joiner, that training has, on numerous occasions, been my fall-back position. Through necessity, I have taught wood machining to disinterested, unruly and, at times, obnoxious kids. I've cleaned second-hand tents, painted houses, filled food shelves for Sainsbury's and taken on shopfitting jobs, work that sometimes required a so-called 'ghost shift' – working all day Saturday then travelling to a distant location to complete a nightshift of shopfitting before returning in the early hours of Sunday morning. For me, this would then mean driving forty miles home to have breakfast before setting off to lead a Sunday morning church gathering.

Like Glenn Holland, there were times when under my breath I have contemplated the fact that, "I never thought I'd be here!"

In terms of biblical characters, however, I find myself in good company.

The Apostle Paul had a 'fall-back position'; it was called 'tent making'. There were times in his life when he needed to revert to his trade of making, repairing and selling tents. Although not his primary purpose in life, 'tent making' was necessary so as 'not to be a burden' on the churches.[129] In this way, Paul financed and facilitated his apostolic ministry through a period of work outside church settings.

A 'fall-back position' is not necessarily a 'set-back position' (as in an act of retreating) but rather a period in which we are prepared to do the menial in order to advance the eternal. This is the Science of the Swing – a backward motion that sets us up for forward momentum. Around the world there is an army of church leaders who are committed to 'tent making' to

---

129. 2 Thessalonians 3:8; Acts 18:1–3; 20:33–35; Philippians 4:14–16.

provide for their family and enable them to build strong local churches. For those who out of necessity find themselves in an unpaid church leadership role, I salute you. You are heroes of the faith who, when exhausted, push forward. When others would retreat, you rally the troops to advance the kingdom in your locality. Your commitment and consistency to further the purpose of God is commendable and should be celebrated.

For me, the seasons of 'tent making' have not been easy. I have needed heaven's help to find God in the waiting time, to keep the main thing the main thing and draw on God's grace to shine both in the spotlight and in the shadows.

I have experienced my own Mr. Holland moments.

This chapter is my backward swing!

Compass People

Having been collared in the school corridor by Principal Jacobs, Mr. Holland is given a brief but barbed assessment as to his initial months as a teacher. Noting the speed and enthusiasm with which he daily sprints to the parking lot after the last period, Principal Jacobs cynically wonders if he would be more suited for the role of a track coach. Dismissing his somewhat defensive response, she then proceeds to outline the characteristics of a good teacher. Good teachers have two tasks. The first is to fill minds with knowledge, the second is to give those minds a compass to ensure that knowledge is not wasted. Uncertain as to what Mr. Holland was doing in the knowledge department, she concluded that as a compass, he was stuck.

**With his opus now gathering dust,
Mr. Holland has no fixed point of reference.**

With no true north, circumstances have cut him adrift. Having lost his way, he is exposed to frustration and discouragement. Unable to point others in the right direction, he risks becoming what in chapter 1 we referred to as an *informer* rather than an *investor* type teacher. In this role he is fast becoming a liability from which his students will one day need to recover, rather than a legacy which one day they will enjoy.

When working in my father's hardware business, I experienced first-hand a person with a 'stuck compass'. In order to provide for his family, a certain Reverend Phelps found himself in a fall-back position. Being a kind-hearted, generous man, my father had offered Mr. Phelps a part-time position in the company. As the pastor of a small struggling inner-city church that had no means of financially supporting him, Mr. Phelps reluctantly accepted my father's offer. With no experience in retail or the building trade, this church leader came to us with little expertise and zero enthusiasm. As someone more use to leading large American churches, becoming a shop assistant was something he never thought he would find himself doing. To Reverend Phelps, this was a visual downgrading from his high and holy calling – and it showed.

A constant annoyance to my brother and me, Mr. Phelps developed what we unkindly referred to as the 'Phelps Shuffle', a slow way of travelling around the store without the soles of his feet ever leaving the beautiful terrazzo tiled shop floor. Add to this his sad demeanour and you begin to envisage how his angle of approach to shop work did little to welcome potential customers. As the doorbell rang to signal a customer entering the store, Mr. Phelps would slowly shuffle from one end of the shop to the other.

Now the less observant might put this down to his age or his somewhat rotund figure. He was not in the first flush of youth, nor in prime physical fitness. But come closing time, both Mr. Phelps's demeanour and walking disability miraculously disappeared. Exiting the store on the strike of six o'clock, he would skip and sprint to the parking lot.

Like Mr. Holland, Mr. Phelps was stuck in a holding pattern waiting for permission to land his dream at his desired destination. Neither man handled their waiting time well. Although these seasons are extremely difficult, they are known as the 'Time Test', a season in which we must learn the lessons of the waiting room or risk having to repeat a year. These are seasons when outward circumstances do not seem to align with God's Word over our lives. Biblical characters like Joseph, Abraham, Moses and Daniel had to find God in the waiting room. It is our attitude, or 'angle of approach' to life in these times that will either cause us to soar or result in a crash and burn. For Mr. Phelps, and initially for Mr. Holland, this waiting time became wasted time.

For Mr. Holland, his teaching credentials were merely a safety net he hoped he would never have to use. What he didn't realise was that sometimes our second option is God's first opportunity. What we believe to be a waste of time can be the time when the Potter's hand moulds us for a future purpose. These are times when, to change the metaphor, the wine-dresser prunes what is good in order to produce what is best. Sometimes, it takes 'the wilderness years' to prepare us for God's 'Promised Land'.

Making the Connection

In this connected, yet disconnected generation, society needs compass people – teachers, parents, peers, mentors, leaders who have found life's true north and are willing to journey with others to direct them towards their God-given purpose in life.

As a malfunctioning compass, Mr. Holland is wandering in the dark with his students. Eventually, his lightbulb moment happens when he chooses to embrace his passion rather than merely educate with his principles. When he does, he exchanges the theory of classical music for the practicality of 1960s pop music. As a result, Glenn Holland makes a critical connection with his class, something in time he will also need to do with his son.

Having made a critical connection with his class, Mr. Holland sets about helping his students find their individual place in the musical score of life. He retunes their discordant lives and enables them to appreciate their individual value in the greater scheme of things. Through three decades of serving his students, many resonate with Mr. Holland's changed approach to teaching. Unknown to Mr. Holland, his teaching career has created a musical masterpiece. Over the course of his working life, his impact and influence on his students have composed a magnum opus – his finest work.

Who knows the domino effect we could be having on those people within our sphere of influence? If I list names like Edward Kimball, Dwight L. Moody, Wilbur Chapman, Billy Sunday, Mordecai Ham you might never have heard of them.

Edward Kimball volunteered his time to connect with a Sunday school class of unruly boys. His personal investment paid dividends in that one of his students called Dwight Moody became a Christ-follower.

Moody in turn introduced Wilbur Chapman to Jesus.

Chapman introduced Billy Sunday to Christianity and Billy, in turn, Mordecai Ham.

It was at one of Ham's evangelistic meeting that a young man called Billy Graham entered a personal relationship with Jesus Christ.

It is reckoned that throughout his life Billy Graham reached an estimated audience of 2.2 billion people. Edward Kimball could never have seen the legacy his life would leave; he was like so many before and since, faithful in the few things.

To begin with, whether it was teaching his class or communicating with his deaf son, Mr. Holland was failing miserably. Having a whole class mess up on a test paper, Holland came to the realisation that despite his best efforts he had made no impact whatsoever. Although his class was physically present, they were mentally and emotionally absent. Mr. Holland was putting in the effort but having zero impact on his audience. Only when he discovered that his students loved Rock & Roll could he find a connection point to engage young minds in his given subject of musical appreciation.

I sometimes wonder if Christianity is making the same mistake by trying to communicate the classical truth to a world hooked on a different genre.

Are we trying to answer questions that no one is asking?

If that's true, then we need to find a way to bridge the communication gap. It's not that we need to change biblical absolutes to accommodate modern thinking, but rather find a common language to reach a post-Christian civilization. Glenn Holland did not have to change the foundational principles of music; he just needed to use a different language. Much of today's younger generations are switching off to our religious platitudes and outdated modes of communication. For those outside the Christian faith, we will need to adopt a more creative approach to communicating the eternal lyrics of a loving Heavenly Father.

However, while Mr. Holland attempted to get to grips with his communication in the classroom, the same cannot be said of his living room and the tense relationship with his son Cole. Personally I find this too close to home for comfort, for "although it might only take a moment to *become* a father, it takes a lifetime of commitment to *be* a Father".[130] The heart-wrenching fact that his son would never be able to hear or appreciate the music he loved is a poignant picture of how many parents feel who would dearly love their children to experience the love of a perfect Heavenly Father. It is truly a tragedy when our kids are deaf to the rhythms of God's amazing grace.

But in all this, maybe we need to find a different way to communicate with those who are spiritually hard of hearing. Shouting louder or using some form of religious sign language will not cut it. Neither will one-off events be enough to communicate God's truth. While Mr. Holland's singing of John Lennon's song, 'Beautiful Boy', to his deaf son was commendable, one-off grand gestures, while emotionally powerful, are not enough.

Sadly, in my meagre effort to communicate the lyrics of heaven with my children, I have tended to get frustrated and either shout louder or use religious sign language, trying to encourage them to appreciate the anthems of heaven. They

---

130. Chris Spicer, *No Perfect Fathers Here*, Chris Spicer, 2010. Emphasis original.

belong to a generation that wants to listen. Tragically, they are being put off by the rants of our archaic religiosity.

If I could have time over again, I would sing over each of my four beautiful children.

I would sing a song over my 'Beautiful Esther' – a star in the heavens shining on earth to show others the way.

'Beautiful Hannah', as gracious by name as by nature!

'Beautiful Luther', who, as his namesake, is a radical reformer, a communicator extraordinaire!

And last but by no means least, 'Beautiful Jonathan', whose pastoral heart watches caringly over those who have no voice of their own.

They are my North, South, East and West, the four corners of my world, those for whom I have always want to be a compass, pointing to life's true north.

Plot Twist

Often, when looking back over our lives, the mind will show us images of mistakes made and opportunities missed. Entertain these images for too long and they will create seepage in our self-esteem. In moments like these, we need to draw on God's grace if we are to find redemption, if we are to buy back the sense of worth that's been stolen.

In one of the finest finales of any movie, Mr. Holland gains a different perspective on his past. In a brilliant piece of theatre, the characters that play out this closing scene give what in storylines terms is known as a *plot twist* – a radical change in the expected direction or outcome of the plot in a book, film or television programme.

To turn a good movie into a great movie, the scriptwriters have been building the plot in order to a play out the conclusion with a magnificent crescendo. This is one of those goose bump moments that sends shivers down my spine no matter how many times I watch it. Mr. Holland's vision of becoming a famous composer is a forgotten dream and his opus a distant memory. But life is about to take a dramatic turn. As someone who has given his life in the service of others, Glenn Holland is preparing to take his final bow in a performance that will, in his mind, soon be forgotten. Believing his life has had little significance in the grand scheme of things, he readies himself to face the final curtain on a thirty-year teaching career. His opus lies silent; fame and fortune have eluded him.

If film endings were to be rated in terms of the number of tissues required, *Dead Poets Society* and *Mr. Holland's Opus* would for me have five stars.

Now in his early sixties, Glenn Holland is about to leave the school for one last time, totally ignorant of the impact and influence his life has made on his students.

Instead of his opus making him famous, he has, unknowingly created a collective masterpiece.

He has composed a magnum opus, his best work.

But it's not a musical score.

It's not a great composition.

It's something else altogether.

Something far more significant.

Those we influence for good are our symphony

The closing scenes of *Mr. Holland's Opus* are among the most moving in film drama. Hundreds of his ex-students and musicians from his thirty-year teaching career have gathered in the school auditorium. Unknown to their teacher, they are waiting there to celebrate Mr. Holland's retirement with the first ever public performance of 'Mr. Hollands Opus'.

When Mr. Holland walks in, the place erupts. Amazed and overwhelmed, he walks through the rousing and passionate ovation. When the applause dies down, his wife stands at the podium and, using sign language so that Mr. Holland's son can understand, introduces the Governor Gertrude Lang, an alumnus of the school, who addresses the crowd. The Governor launches into a praiseworthy account of Mr. Holland's music teaching career. She speaks of the profound influence Mr. Holland has had on both her and all those gathered in that auditorium. Addressing the retiree, she speaks of how although he might feel his life has been misspent and achieved little, he has achieved a fame far greater than he will ever know.

Governor Lang then explains the reason for an orchestra of present and past students seated on the stage. Mr. Holland, she continues, has been working on a symphony, which he hoped one day might make him rich and famous, but sadly Mr. Holland is neither. Yet although he might perceive himself as a failure, he would be mistaken. Each and every person in this auditorium is here today because of you, she explains. And then in one of those goose bump moments, Governor Gertrude Lang, herself a proficient flautist, declares to Mr. Holland that the people there are the notes of his grand opus and that they are the music that has poured out of his life.

Now that's a speech! And that's also a great metaphor.

What a great description of a musician's legacy!

"We are your symphony."

However, the film is not done, and the tears are not yet dry either. Mr Holland is invited to the stage to conduct the first ever performance of his magnum opus, with the governor even playing clarinet in the orchestra!

And so, the film ends.

Mr. Holland gets to perform *The American Symphony* after all.

His wife and son look proudly on, aware perhaps for the first time of the pain and struggle he had to bear, the extraordinary gifts and passion he had always possessed, and the love and estimation of so many he had taught.

In the end, Mr. Holland realised that his greatest *opus* was the people he had taught more than the music he had composed. They were his legacy and he needed to come to see that for himself, and that's the epiphany to which the whole story leads.

My Father's Opus

My own father could have so easily mirror-imaged the mindset of Mr. Holland. If asked, he would probably say that his life had little lasting impact. But he would be wrong. If my father were here, I would say to him, "Look around Dad, there are generations reaching their potential because of you. Ministers, businesspeople, social entrepreneurs, teachers, mothers, fathers, children around the world are living in the legacy you left." My father worked day and night to build a family business, which he hoped to leave as a legacy for his two sons. Believing his decision was God-given, he began it in the appalling economic climate of post-war Britain. Most working-class families were coping with penny-pinching austerity rather than enjoying the prosperity of the swinging 60s just around the corner.

Sinking every penny he had and could borrow from family and friends, he began his risky venture.

Eventually, my elder brother would inherit the business while I chose a different path, something my father never fully understood.

In terms of a legacy, the successful business that took my father a quarter of a century to build has long since disappeared. The name 'Spicer's Hardware' is just a distant memory spoken by an ageing population who still recall a friendly family business that would do anything to help its customers. But like Mr. Holland's, my father's legacy is a far greater than anything he could have thought possible. Today, grandchildren and great-grandchildren carry a torch for biblical truth because of that initial investment of time, energy and resources he made into the business. His magnum opus still resounds a quarter of a century after his death.

When my local church wanted to buy a property to extend its existing premises, the owners were adamant that they would never under any circumstance sell their building to Christians, no matter how polite or pushy they might be. However, during the negotiations in which my nephew was involved, somehow the owners heard the surname 'Spicer'. Enquiring of my nephew if he was in anyway related to Mr. Thomas Spicer of Spicer's Hardware, he answered, "Yes, he was my granddad!" At that moment the whole negotiation took a radical turn for the better. Evidently, Thomas Spicer had been a customer when the owners of the building ran a home décor business from these premises. They recalled the kind-hearted, gentle spirit of an honest man with whom it was a pleasure to do business. The building was purchased at a reasonable price and today it is part of social outreach of Mosaic Church and the City of Coventry.

In terms of all the hard work and his dream of leaving his sons a legacy, my father's opus was not fully realised. But while his temporal legacy did not last, his eternal legacy lives on.

Whether we like it or not, our lives will be a chapter in the autobiography of others. Today, we plough a furrow in which others will follow.

The question is, will it be *a legacy to rejoice in or a liability to recover from?* For some, that legacy will not be what they imagined. For others it might not be seen in their lifetime. The fame and fortune they had hoped for, their influence and impact on those they have invested in will go further, reach higher and delve deeper than they could have ever dreamed.

One day, people will say of us, "We are your symphony."

And that's the best of all legacies.

KEEPING IT REEL

Mistakes I Have Made:
- Looking for too long in the rear-view mirror.
- Answering questions no one is asking.
- Hoping the one-off grand gesture will communicate a father's love.
- Having a wrong attitude to 'tent making'.
- Missing the point.

Lessons I Have Learnt:
- To become a compass person.
- Change the channel but not the content of my communication.
- The legacy I leave may not look like the one I'd hoped for.
- People not possessions are the best legacy.
- It may take generations before my legacy is realised.

EPILOGUE

Don't be a Muppet

Hands up those who recognise the following television personalities: Rowlf the Dog; Rizzo the Rat; Fozzie Bear; The Great Gonzo; Miss Piggy or Kermit the Frog! No?! Well that's good, because it probably means that you weren't around in the 1970s and as such makes you an ideal candidate to have read this book.

For the uninitiated, this list of characters comes from a 1970s television programme, *The Muppet Show*. Brainchild of the entrepreneurial genius Jim Henson, this family-orientated puppet show was essential primetime viewing with its music-hall style, slapstick comedy, and song-and-dance routines. A protagonist puppet by the name of Kermit the Frog was given the role of hosting twenty-six minutes of weekly mayhem. As well as the unenviable task of keeping his fellow Muppets in some sort of order, Kermit tried his best to keep a long list of human celebrities happy. With guest celebrities like Steve Martin, Liza Minnelli, Julie Andrews, Elton John and Alice Cooper (more names you probably won't recognise), *The Muppet Show* fast became the not-to-be-missed TV programme of the late seventies.

Although some fans would think differently, Kermit the Frog was arguably Jim Henson's most famous puppet creation. Others say it's Miss Piggy, with her volatile diva style, a tendency to use French phrases and practise karate; others, the Great Gonzo, with his eccentric passion for performing stunts, or Animal, the crazy drummer, or Rowlf the Dog, the wacky pianist.

For me, however, the prize is reserved for two Muppets who never actually appeared on stage.

For those who prefer their humour with a tinge of sarcasm, the two characters known as Statler and Waldorf would probably be your Muppets of choice. Named after two New York hotels, these two elderly puppets had characteristically promoted themselves to the role of show critics. From the comfort of their boxed balcony seats, these two cantankerous individuals would constantly heckle the performance of their fellow Muppets. This variety show, with its outrageous physical slapstick and absurd comedy, rarely went to plan – something these two side-line critics took great pleasure in pointing out. To add insult to injury, Statler and Waldorf would characteristically sign off each performance with some cryptic comments like:

STATLER:

"Well, they say that all good things come to an end!"

WALDORF:

"What's that got to do with this show?"

Offering little in the way of personal encouragement, these two ageing hecklers preferred to sit back and criticise the efforts of their younger and somewhat inexperienced counterparts.

What a picture that is!

Like no other time in history, Western civilization is having to play host to an ageing population – a post-war generation that is living long enough to observe how their offspring handle the inheritance for which they worked hard to achieve. Sitting comfortably in homes bought and paid for, many so-called 'Baby Boomers' are enjoying a financial freedom for which their children can only dream. As senior citizens they have a choice. They can either sit back and bemoan the efforts of their offspring, or step up to the plate and applaud those who now find themselves centre stage of businesses, churches and social enterprises that a previous generation created. The older generation has a choice whether they are going to *cheer* or *jeer* the efforts of those trying their best to make the world a better place.

The Changeover Box

Although the dialogue between Waldorf, Statler and the rest of the cast is entertaining, it also serves to showcase a generational challenge primed to explode. Builders, Boomers, Busters and Bridgers/Millennials are generational groups that have, over the last hundred years, shaped Western culture.[131] The strengths and weaknesses of each of these generations have contributed to the ongoing success or failure of society. But there comes a time, as in an Olympic relay race, when the baton must be handed to others.

That time is now.

---

131. Builders – 1925–1945; Boomers – 1946–1964; Busters – 1965–1983; Bridgers – 1980–1990; Millennials – 1991–2018.

This critical moment in a relay race is known as the Changeover Box – a 20 metre section of track in which two runners position themselves to either release or receive the baton. Whereas one has completed their race, the other will continue what their predecessors began. More relay runners mess up in the Changeover Box than at any other part of the race. Races are won and lost in this section of track. It is here that two runners must get up to speed and position themselves ready for the handover of a piece of aluminium tube.

The modern Olympic relay race originates from ancient Aboriginals who used runners to carry messages between tribes.

In this way, legends were passed from one tribe to another, from one generation to another.

When a message needed to be carried over a long distance, a group of runners would be used, thereby ensuring the speed and safe arrive of an important piece of information. However, in the ancient world a dropped message could easily be retrieved, and the intended recipient would still receive the prize.

Not so in the Olympic games.

What makes the Changeover Box so challenging is that the handoff is usually done blind. While the lead runner is reaching backwards to take hold of the baton, both runners must get up to speed while sharing the same space. In a miniscule moment of time, both have hold of the baton, but while the receiver must grasp it, the releaser must make sure they do not let the baton go too soon or hold on for too long – all this while running at speeds of up to 20 mph.

While some individuals like the Waldorfs and Statlers criticise the present, others believe their role in life is to preserve the past. Rather than celebrating the past and enabling the present, they become a 'Muppet' who insists on holding tightly onto what has clearly passed its sell-by-date. This is foolish.

Don't Stuff the Dead Dog

Never Have Your Dog Stuffed is the catchy title of Alan Alda's autobiography, in which he uses his wry sense of humour to record a number of life lessons from his childhood. The title comes from a tragic, but somewhat humorous story surrounding the death of his pet dog called Rhapsody. When Alan was inconsolable after the dog's death, his father tried to comfort his son by promising that Rhapsody would return. Unknown to Alan, his Dad went and asked the local taxidermist to work his magic on the canine corpse. However, the taxidermist had never seen the animal alive. Needless to say, the man's efforts to reinstate the past were somewhat out of tune with reality.

On Rhapsody's return, it soon became clear that in seeking to preserve the past, the ill-advised taxidermist had created a monster: "We pulled off the brown butcher's paper he was wrapped in and looked at him. The dog had a totally unrecognisable expression on his face. He looked as if he'd seen something loathsome that needed to be shredded."

He concluded, "Losing the dog wasn't as bad as getting him back!"

Visiting family had to be forewarned that the dog in the living room was not real. The canine's vicious looks convinced people that he was in desperate need of human flesh. Even when demoted to the porch, deliverymen would do anything to avoid the house.

Rhapsody became a constant reminder that things would never again be the way they were. "I see now," writes Alda, "that stuffing your dog is what happens when you hold on to any living thing a moment longer than it wants you to."[132]

---

132. Alan Alda, *Never Have Your Dog Stuffed*, Arrow, 2007.

To preserve the past, how often do we create a facsimile, a scary monster that does little to attract people to our group or organisation?

Holding onto something longer than it wants us to can seriously affect our ability to move forward and possess the future.

Kodak's inability to embrace the future offered by Polaroid is seen by some as a mistake that would ultimately lead to their demise.

Xerox had everything in their business development department to make the Apple Mac, but it took a forward-thinking Steve Jobs to bring about this innovative breakthrough in the world of personal computers.

Many publishers rejected the Harry Potter story before a small publishing house called Bloomsbury had an editor whose 8-year-old daughter asked for the author not to take the book back as she wanted to finish it. The rest, as they say, is publishing history.

Vibrant organisations can quickly become living museums when a minority chooses to exercise mental taxidermy on old methodology. To succeed in an ever-changing society, we will need mental agility, the ability to adapt to a new way of doing things. When an older generation insists on preserving the past instead of securing the future, then we run the risk of trying to stuff the dead dog. Having acknowledged what is good from the past, we need to plant it in such a way that it fertilises the future. We cannot give room to the monsters that my generation might inadvertently create. Those who cheer rather than jeer the younger generation must make room for the 'puppies' of innovation and enterprise.

They must heed this author's cry, *"Don't be a Muppet!"*

It's a Wrap!

The Reel Story, like most movies, is a visual narration involving one main character. That's because movies are like life. Screenwriters, actors, directors and producers use different currency to increase a film's entertainment value – exotic locations, historic scenery, beautiful costumes, incredible cinematography and magnificent musical scores. With various twists and turns along the way, a cast of characters will create a visual masterpiece and tug at the heartstrings. While some stories will cause us to cry tears of joy, others will submerge us in a sea of sorrow. The unexpected will hold us in suspense and have us sitting on the edge of our seats, while the unexplained will leave us confused and begging for answers. True greatness lies in a film's ability to take us out of our difficult circumstances to another world.

But that's life!

We sit in silent anticipation with little idea of what is about to unravel. Although we might prefer our story to have a classic beginning and a fairy tale ending, the truth is, our beginnings can be messy and our endings unpredictable. Unlike movies, our stories don't fall neatly into one simple category. Life is a mixture of comedy, fantasy, romance, tragedy, and so on. Although we might struggle with the ups and downs of life, whatever happens, we're here now. We have a vested interest in the life being played out before us, and no matter how rough it gets we must remain seated in the truth of who we are in Christ Jesus. We need to play our part, fulfil the role designated for us, for sooner or later heaven's director will call time and say, "It's a wrap!"

When, as a teenager, I surrendered my life to a loving Heavenly Father, I had no idea how my movie would play out. Although certain aspects of my life I would have preferred to be left on the cutting room floor, the truth is, this has been the adventure of a lifetime. Although my greatest legacy is my four children, my prayer is that my life will leave a *legacy* in which others will rejoice, rather than a *liability* from which they will need to recover. As I continue to pursue life in the last lane, my hope is that *The Reel Story* will encourage the next generation to go further and faster than my generation ever thought possible.

So, using Porky Pig's famous signoff, this really is all folks. Apart from rolling the credits, we have come to the end of this performance. It's now in hands of the critics.

Hopefully, no animals or humans were harmed in the writing of this book.

The End

Chris Spicer is a leader with over fifty years' experience working with Christian communities and learning centres throughout Europe and North America. Having lived in Portland, Oregon and Peoria, Illinois, Chris now lives in England. Chris and his wife Tina have four adult children and eight rock-star grandchildren. Public speaker and published author, Chris's other titles include: *No Perfect Fathers Here*; *JJ & the Big Bend* and *Life on the Hill*.

Credits

It goes without saying that my family would top this list. For those people I have worked with over years who are not mentioned in this list, the reason is simple, "I don't like you!" – just joking. These names are just a few of the people who over a seventy-year period have in some way had a positive influence on my life.

Tina Spicer – My Constant Companion

Revd George Waring – Founding Father

Robert Barrowclough – Revelatory Teacher

Mr. Jenkins – Inspirational High School Teacher

Mrs. Smith – Patient Piano Teacher

Robert Winters – Woodwork Mentor

Jim Elliot – Fire Lighter

John Phillips – Prince of Preachers

Dave Lakin – World's Best Children's Worker

Roger Blackmore, Ian Jennings,
Ken Hudson, Alan Penduck, Peter Butt,
Pasquarle Barcellona – Bible College Buddies

Revd Aaron Morgan – Lecturer Par excellence

John Poole – Preaching Tutor

Eric Lavender – A Friend at Midnight

Dick Iverson – Apostolic Father

Ern Baxter – Eye Opener

Richard Robinson & Bill Nesbit – Fun Work Colleagues

Hugh Thompson – Bible Teacher Extraordinaire

Graham Deakin – Pastor Par excellence

Joff Day – Entrepreneurial Go-Getter

Andy Owen – True Pioneer

Alan & Karan Skyles – Life Changers

Dr. Martin Luther King – Prophet of Peace

Adrian Hurst – The Grace Man

Major Howdy Byron Sligar Jr. – Mr. Amen

John King – Welsh Prophet

J. D. Walt – Breath of Fresh Air

Chris Sutton – Forerunner of Eternity

Gary Spicer – One who Fails Forward

Bishop Tony Miller – God's Spokesman

Mark Jarvis – My Parachute Packer